The Summer Assembly Book

The Summer
Assembly Book

REDVERS BRANDLING

SIMON & SCHUSTER
EDUCATION

First published in 1993 in Great Britain by
Simon & Schuster Education
Campus 400, Maylands Avenue
Hemel Hempstead, Herts HP2 7EZ

British Library Cataloguing in Publication Data is
available on request from the British Library

ISBN 0 7501 0619 0

Set in 11/13pt Times by
Derek Doyle & Associates, Mold, Clwyd
Printed in the United Kingdom by
T.J. Press, Padstow

Contents

Section B: class assemblies linked to significant times in the term 151

Section C: anniversaries, facts, fancies, anecdotes, religious notes for every day of the summer term 173

Section D: assemblies linked by theme 195

Animals, Concern, Courage, Environment,
Faith, Friendship, Guidance, Heroes and Heroines, Home,
Journeys, Living Together, Ourselves, Senses,
Those Who help Us

Section E: the stories 199

Folk stories, myths, legends
True stories
Religious stories
Original or contemporary stories

Section F: National Curriculum cross-references 201

Art
English
Geography
History
Mathematics
Music
Physical Education
Science
Technology

Section G: resources 205

Acknowledgements

I am, as always, grateful to the staff and children of Dewhurst St Mary School, Cheshunt. They have been a receptive audience for all the material in this book, and a source of both inspiration and information with their own presentations.

The material supplied to schools from Save the Children and the Christian Education Movement has been of great value. Of the many anthologies referred to, *Folk tales of India* and *Folk Tales of the World* (both published by Sterling) have been especially valuable.

It should also be mentioned that some of the stories in this book have been used, heard and re-adapted several times in assemblies. In consequence their original sources are not remembered and if this has unwittingly caused the infringement of copyright, the author apologises and will correct this omission in future editions, if notified.

Introduction

'Effective assembly occasions take a great deal of time to prepare.'[1]

'Assemblies must contain a sense of expectancy, a willingness to co-operate, some unity between those present by reason of shared experiences or common values.'[2]

'In achieving this meaningful act . . . other means . . . are valid . . . stories and readings; dance and drama; prayer/meditation; creative silence; songs/hymns/music; sacred/secular readings; artefacts and natural materials; children's contributions; visual aids.'[3]

These quotations effectively reinforce what all those who take even an occasional assembly already know. Apart from its being a mandatory daily requirement, the primary school assembly should at all times be well presented, thoughtful, reflective, and involve the children. For ever-increasingly busy Heads and teachers it is therefore an extremely demanding task.

This is the third of three books comprising material for the autumn, spring and summer terms. It seeks to provide constructive, practical help for a complete summer term of assemblies.

It begins with a series of ready-made assemblies for each month – nine for April, and seventeen each for May, June and July. This gives a total of sixty assemblies which are 'instant' in that they provide an introduction, story, suggested hymn and prayer. They also, however, contain sections on 'Information for the teacher' and 'National Curriculum cross-curricular reference'. The use of these will hopefully enhance each assembly and, as with any ready-made material, reflection and preparation beforehand add enormously to its potential.

The second section in the book contains a number of class assemblies. Once again these are prepared in a detailed manner – aims, materials required, calendar locations, numbers involved,

---

[1] *Themes for Assembly*, S Brimer (Blackie and Son)
[2] *First School Religious Education*, T and G Copley (SCM Press)
[3] *Collective Worship in Hertfordshire*, Guidance for schools.

preparation, information, presentation – and contain a variety of playscripts. The latter are reproduced in large print so that they can be used for photocopying and group involvement.

Section C contains an anniversary, fact, fancy or anecdote for every day in the spring term. Many of these are ideal starting material for other assemblies and interspersed with them are notes referring to ready-made assemblies elsewhere in the book. Where this is the case links of ideas or themes offer further expansion possibilities.

For teachers who do not wish to use the assemblies chronologically and prefer a thematic approach, Sections D and E aim to help in this context. Section D groups assemblies into popular primary school themes – *animals, concern, courage*, etc. Section E links the assemblies by their source – *folk, true, religious, original*, etc.

Section F acknowledges that many teachers now feel that assembly material should be linked to other areas of the National Curriculum. This is done here by identifying other National Curriculum subjects and linking assembles to them where appropriate.

The final section in the book provides details of resources.

Redvers Brandling

Section A
Complete assemblies

April

1 The mystery

Introduction

Have you ever noticed that when somebody does something bad, it often brings the best out of somebody else? This morning's story is about a mystery which was never solved – and it is also about courage, skill and determination.

Story

'You can now unfasten your seatbelts, and I wish you a smooth and comfortable flight.'

The voice of Captain Ian Harvey filled the cabin of the airliner as it reached its cruising height and settled on course. It flew through the night, which was lit by occasional flashes of lightning, and the passengers settled down to enjoy a meal.

For stewardess Sue Cramsie this was a busy time.

'I expect they're all as hungry as ever,' she thought as she handed round the trays of food. 'Funny though – there seems to be a peculiar smell around.'

As she sniffed again, Sue felt a chill of fear run up her back. The smell was of something burning! She hurried to the back of the plane to investigate, but she never got there. Just as she turned there was a blinding explosion, the cabin filled with smoke and Sue was hurled unconscious to the floor.

'We're going to crash!' yelled one of the passengers.

'Keep calm,' shouted another.

'The girl . . . ' gasped a third, as the smoke cleared and revealed a terrifying sight. On each side of the aircraft's cabin there was a huge hole, and lying dangerously near to both of them was the unconscious stewardess.

'Let's get her to safety,' said one of the passengers quietly, and two men dragged Sue to a safer position.

Meanwhile, up in the cockpit, Captain Harvey and his co-pilot, First

Officer Dusty Miller, were struggling to keep the aircraft from falling out of the sky. The explosion had taken them completely by surprise and had seriously damaged the controls.

'Dusty,' gasped Captain Harvey, 'get back there and see what the problems are. I'll try and hold her.'

Sweat poured down Captain Harvey's face as he held the bucking, almost unbearably heavy control column. Without a word, First Officer Miller got up and went to investigate. He was back, grim faced, within a couple of minutes.

'It's not good,' he said. 'Half the control rods have gone, there's two whacking great holes in the fuselage and the tail's hanging on by a whisker. Sue's hurt and unconscious but there's no panic. The passengers are looking after her.'

'Right,' said Ian Harvey. 'We're going back to London. Radio now – say we're badly damaged, stewardess seriously injured, have emergency services standing by.'

With desperate care, Captain Harvey turned the plane back towards London. Lurching and groaning through the sky, it wallowed in the night until the runway lights came into view. Strapped in and tense, the passengers watched the lights get nearer and nearer – and then with a sudden screaming of engines the plane lifted into the sky again.

'She nearly stalled that time,' shouted Captain Harvey. 'We'll try again.'

This time, despite all the problems, the damaged plane touched down smoothly on the runway. Sue was rushed to hospital in an ambulance, and the calm and brave passengers were shepherded to safety.

Then Captain Harvey, First Officer Miller and some ground staff experts carefully inspected the damaged plane. It was a miracle that it had ever got back to the ground and only a brilliant pilot could have helped it to do so.

At first it was thought that the plane had been struck by lightning, but a later inspection showed that the explosion had been caused by a bomb somebody had put on board.

Who had done so, and why, has remained a mystery. What is not a mystery is that on that terrifying night, everybody aboard aircraft G-AIVL had behaved in the best possible way. Sue Cramsie made a complete recovery and was soon back at work.

Information for the teacher

1   This incident occurred on 13th April 1950. The aircraft was a BEA

Viking, and the flight was from London to Paris. Captain Harvey had previously been a distinguished bomber pilot in the Second World War, and his skill and courage on this occasion received great publicity. The explosive device had been planted in the towel compartment in the toilet.

2 A few appropriate books from the school's reference library could make a useful hall display to enhance this assembly. There are various books on pilots and air hostesses but a good 'basic' reference book is *Working at an airport* by Edwina Cox, published by Wayland.

3 British Airways materials for schools (booklets/film strips) can be obtained from Visual Publications, 197 Kensington High Street, London W8 6BB.

Hymn suggestion

Come and Praise Vol 2 'You've got to move' No 197

Prayer

Let us pray this morning for all those people who drive buses, steer ships, pilot aeroplanes, drive trains.

Let us pray for all those people who work in transport and let us give thanks for their skill and experience which keep passengers safe. Amen.

National Curriculum Cross Curricular Reference

This is a very dramatic story that could be acted out in various ways in the classroom. It also provides discussion material for older primary children.

'Flight' is a very popular Science topic and this is probably the strongest area for integration.

2   The tooth

Introduction

Do you remember when you started school – how lonely and worried you felt? Of course, lots of other children felt the same and you probably soon made friends. It's a bit different when you change schools and everybody knows everyone else – except you.

Story

Assundra kept her eyes down on the book's page. She wasn't reading it though, she was listening.

'Are you going to Brownies tonight?'

'Yes – it's going to be something special, Brown Owl says.'

'Jackie Bence's big brother's got a new colour telly in his bedroom.'

'My mum says I can stay up as late as I like if I'm working on my computer.'

So it went on. Everybody chatting, everybody saying something – except Assundra. Nobody said anything to her, so she didn't dare interrupt and say anything herself.

Worriedly, she poked her teeth with her tongue again. Then, suddenly, she was no longer aware of what the voices were saying. Her tooth! It began wobbling backwards and forwards, and then, with a sort of little click, it came away from her gum. She put up a hand and took it from her mouth. Around her the voices stopped for a minute, and then they all started again, as if at once.

'Assundra – your tooth's come out!'

'You lucky devil – get it under your pillow tonight.'

'That tooth fairy was worth 50p when mine came out last week.'

'Doesn't it feel funny where the tooth used to be, 'Sundra?'

'Here, let's have a look.'

Assundra felt herself go hot and cold. She had forgotten all about the tooth.

'They're talking to me,' she thought. 'And they're calling me by my name.'

She felt a warm feeling spread over her.

'Think I'll see if there's any more loose,' she said, pressing her teeth with her finger.

There was a burst of laughter from the other girls.

'Oh – she's going to be rich, this girl,' one of them joked.

Information for the teacher

1   Guru Nanak, the founder of the Sikh religion, was someone who advocated kindness and consideration to all. Several stories about him illustrate this, and he was born on 15th April 1469.

Thus this calendar link could be used to integrate this story – and also to provide a thought-provoking quotation. Guru Nanak was once criticised by a Muslim because he slept with his feet towards Mecca. He replied, 'If you think it is wrong for me to point my feet towards the house of God, show me some direction in which God does not dwell.'

2 This assembly could easily lead on to others of a similar nature, devised by the children themselves. 'How I made friends' could yield a selection of true incidents which would make good assembly material – and provoke useful discussion afterwards.

Hymn suggestion

Come and Praise Vol 1 'When I needed a neighbour' No 65

Prayer

Dear God,
Help us to be aware of everyone's needs for friendship. Let us not wait for others to be kind to children who are new and lonely. Teach us to be welcoming and generous. Amen.

National Curriculum Cross Curricular Reference

Whilst this is predominantly a theme for greater expansion in RE, it offers good opportunities for English work. Primary children can usually write very well (in both poems and prose) on the topic of 'friends'. There is also much scope for discussion and drama.

3 *Jonah*

Introduction

All of us know the feeling that there is something we should do – but don't want to. This morning's story is a very old one. It is about a man who had a job to do but tried to get out of it. He certainly learned his lesson as a result!

Story

Jonah was God's messenger. One day God said to him, 'Go to the city of Nineveh and tell the people there to change their evil ways.'

Jonah was shocked. Nineveh was the capital of the great empire of Assyria and Jonah was frightened about what might happen to him if he went to do this job.

'They're cruel people there,' he thought. 'They won't listen to me and they could throw me in prison or even kill me. I'll just pretend to go.'

So Jonah went to the docks, but instead of boarding a ship to take him to Nineveh he got on one which was going in the opposite direction.

'God will never know where I have gone,' he thought to himself.

He was wrong. A day out of port, the ship ran into a terrible storm. Huge waves crashed over it, tearing away the rigging and threatening to capsize the ship at any second. The sailors worked like madmen. In the screaming wind, they fought with what was left of the sails and they even hurled some of the cargo overboard to lighten the ship. Nothing made any difference. The wind blew with ever-increasing force and the waves rose higher and higher. The captain asked Jonah to pray to his God, but of course this made no difference.

'It's no good,' said Jonah. 'I think this is all happening because of me. You see, I was supposed to go and do a job and . . . well . . . I've tried to get out of it.'

He then told the captain the whole story. When he had finished, he asked the captain to throw him overboard.

'I can't do that!' gasped the captain. 'What we'll do is row the ship into the shore and let you off.'

So the sailors tried to do this. The mast and sails were now all gone and the ship could only be kept under control by being rowed. Still the storm raged all round it.

'Don't worry, Jonah, we'll soon have you safe!' called one of the sailors as the water streamed down his tired face.

He was wrong. As soon as the ship headed towards the shore the storm got even worse. Oars snapped like matchsticks and the crew were knee-deep in the water which thundered over the sides of the boat.

'You've got to throw me overboard – now!' yelled Jonah above the tumult. Reluctantly, the terrified sailors took his arms and legs and hurled him into the raging sea.

As Jonah hit the water, two things happened. The storm died at once and the ship settled calmly. Secondly, a passing whale opened its huge mouth and swallowed Jonah, despite his struggles. By a miracle, however, he survived and was eventually washed up safely on the shore. There, exhausted and wiser, he lay recovering his strength.

'How foolish I've been,' he thought. 'I should have known I could never run away from what God wants me to do.'

So he began to prepare for his journey to Nineveh.

Information for the teacher

1 The consequences of 'not doing what we know we should do' offer plenty of opportunity for supplementary material for this assembly – the mechanic who doesn't service a car properly, the builder who builds a sub-standard house, the teacher who doesn't prepare a lesson, etc, etc.

2 For those who wish to refer in more detail to the Biblical source of this story, the reference is Jonah 1, 1–17.

   It is interesting that in some symbolic interpretations of this story the sea stands for 'world politics!'

3 Another feature which this story emphasises is the courage and determination of sailors in the most extreme danger. This is another topic which could be followed up with plenty of more modern examples which are well documented.

4 There are plenty of sea-related April calendar anniversaries to which this story could be linked. Isambard Kingdom Brunel, builder of the *Great Western* (the first ship to provide a regular transatlantic service, in 1843) and the *Great Eastern* (the largest ship to be built up to that time, in 1858) was born on 9th April 1806. Robert Watson-Watt, the Scottish inventor of RADAR, was born on the 13th, in 1892. The *Titanic* sank on the 15th, in 1912. John Franklin, discoverer of the North West Passage, was born on the 16th, in 1786. Joshua Slocum set sail from Boston, USA, on 24th April 1895 to make the first single-handed voyage round the world in the nine-ton sloop *Spray*; it took him three and a quarter years.

Hymn suggestion

Come and Praise Vol 2 'Make us worthy' No 94

Prayer

Dear God,

Give us the strength that we may do those things which we know we should do. Help us to avoid laziness, carelessness and fear and guide us so that we always do a job as well as we possibly can. Amen.

National Curriculum Cross Curricular Reference

Locating where this story is set is a useful geographical exercise which could be linked with locating other great seas and oceans. The causes and effects of storms could further this work and link it with Science.

A study of sailing ships could incorporate History and Technology and the vigour and fear of a 'storm at sea' could provoke both poetry and some improvised musical experiments. The latter could be supported by listening to some suitable recorded material – the overture to Wagner's *The Flying Dutchman*, or Debussy's *La Mer*, for example.

4   *A day out*

Introduction

I expect most of you know how much your grandparents like a day out. For some people one of the most enjoyable ways of spending a day like this is to go on a coach outing . . .

Story

'It's great – just look at that view of the sea.'

'In ten minutes we're going to stop down there for a cup of tea.'

'Did you bring a picnic, Betty?'

Colin Henry smiled. He was driving a big, fifty-seater coach. Behind him he could hear people chatting – saying the same sort of things they always said on outings like this.

'As long as they enjoy it,' he thought, 'that's what it's all about.'

He thought about the busy streets of Liverpool, where most of his passengers came from, and the lovely seaside views of Devon they were looking at now. He had made this journey so often that he didn't really need to think about it.

Suddenly, a feeling of terror crept up the back of Colin's neck and made his skin prickle with fear.

'No, I must be wrong,' he thought, and eased his right foot down once again on the brake pedal. But again he had that sickening feeling that there was nothing there – his brakes really had failed!

'I've got to try and hide it as long as I can,' thought Colin as the coach began to pick up speed on its descent into the seaside town of Paignton.

Faster and faster and faster it went. Now the driver could no longer pretend. It took all his skill and strength to hang onto the steering wheel as the runaway vehicle swayed and screeched round the downhill corners. All conversation had stopped and the white-faced passengers gripped the seats in front of them as they were flung from side to side.

Sweat poured down Colin's forehead as he sought to control the coach, and at the same time find some way to stop. Then, among the houses which flashed by, he saw one ahead that was obviously empty – it was now or never.

'Hang on!' shouted Colin and aimed his coach at the empty house. A telegraph pole which stood in the way was smashed to pieces and the vehicle ploughed into the front wall.

There was a momentary pause, and then . . . whoosh! – flames and smoke began to leap out of the engine compartment.

Next door to the empty house lived Maurice Ildster. Shocked and frightened by the terrific noise, he dashed out of his house and saw the wrecked coach and the spreading flames. Instantly he returned inside and came back with a fire extinguisher.

'It's OK, I'm coming,' he yelled. Racing up to the coach, he began to fight the spreading flames. Within seconds his prompt action had put the fire out. Throwing down the extinguisher, Maurice then began to help the shocked and shaken passengers out of the coach. Miraculously, not one of them was seriously hurt.

The emergency services had now been alerted and next on the scene was a fire engine. Poor Colin the driver was trapped in his cabin and had to be cut out. Soon he was on his way to hospital with back injuries.

'It was a miracle,' said one of the passengers, Mrs Betty McCarron, a little while later. 'But for the courage and skills of our wonderful driver, and the quick thinking of the young man with the fire extinguisher, I'm sure most of us would have been killed.'

Information for the teacher

1   This incident took place on 17th April 1992 in Paignton. The driver of the coach was Colin Henry, aged forty-two, and his elderly passengers were all from the Maghull area of Liverpool and at the start of a day trip. The hero with the fire extinguisher was Maurice Ildster, a thirty-five-year-old soldier.

2   The sense of 'movement and fire' could be enhanced by some appropriate recorded music for this assembly. Two suggestions are *Ritual Fire Dance* by Falla, and Stravinsky's *Firebird Suite*.

3   For background information on roads, traffic and transport, a

useful address for teachers is: British Road Federation, 388–396 Oxford Street, London W1N 9HE.

For more details on fires and fire protection, a useful address is: Fire Protection Association, 140 Aldersgate Street, London EC1A 4HY.

Hymn suggestion

Come and Praise Vol 1 'Travel On' No 42

Prayer

Let us pray for all those who are making journeys today on land, sea or in the air. May they reach their destinations safely. Amen.

National Curriculum Cross Curricular Reference

Wheels, brakes and fire are all topics which can include research and practical work in Science and Technology. This particular incident is one which lends itself readily to drama. A historical feature might be to study the history of road transport, or more specifically, the history of buses. Music could be involved in the assembly – see point 2 above.

5   Trust in Allah

Introduction

This morning's story is about the adventures of three men. Two of them were dissatisfied and wanted more; the third was a man who was grateful for what he had. This is what happened to them . . .

Story

The three friends had been on a long, tiring journey. They were desperate for a rest.

'Look,' said Haroun, 'there's a garden. It looks inviting and quiet. Let's camp there for the night.'

'An excellent idea,' agreed Anim.

Abdul, the third of the friends, was already looking for a spot where he could light a fire to cook the evening meal.

An hour later, the fire was blazing merrily. The friends had eaten well and were relaxing and talking before they went to bed.

Now, what they did not know was that this garden belonged to a king, and his palace overlooked the garden. Some time ago the king had told his gardener that he didn't want any more fires lit in the garden. Now, looking out of his palace windows, he saw the flickering firelight.

'That gardener,' he muttered furiously to himself. 'How dare he light a fire and disobey my orders.'

Stopping only to wrap himself in a long cloak, the king left the palace and hurried to the garden. As he got near to the fire he saw the three friends. Intrigued, he stopped, hid behind a tree and listened to what they were saying.

'Money – that's what life is all about,' Haroun said. 'If you are rich, life's no problem. I wish, above all else, that I was rich.'

'No, no,' replied Anim. 'What you want is a wife to look after you. Then you've got no worries – you've got good food and a comfortable house. I'm fed up of life the way it is. I wish I had a woman to look after me.'

Adbul smiled.

'You're too discontented, my friends,' he said. 'Allah provides everything we need. We have to thank him for everything.'

The other two continued to moan and grumble in the same way.

Meanwhile, the king listened carefully, and then, as quietly as he had come, he slipped back to the palace.

Early next morning he had the three men arrested and brought before him.

'Last night you trespassed in my garden.'

'We didn't know, Your Majesty,' said the three frightened friends.

'What's more,' went on the king, 'I know every word you said. Tell me your words. If you speak the truth I will reward you; if you lie I will have you executed.'

Terrified, the three friends repeated their conversation.

'Right,' said the king, pointing to Haroun. 'You shall have the treasure you desire so much.'

So saying, he clapped his hands, and Haroun was given a huge sack of treasure.

'And you,' went on the king, indicating Anim, 'shall have my daughter as your wife.'

At this a princess bowed low, and joined the astonished Anim.

'And as for you,' snapped the king, pointing at Abdul, 'you can just carry on waiting to see how your God looks after you.'

Two hours later, the friends were on their way again. They still hadn't recovered from their surprise – but Haroun was already moaning again.

'This bag is so heavy,' he grumbled. 'Abdul, will you carry it a while for me?'

'Of course,' replied Abdul, heaving the sack of treasure onto his shoulders.

Just at that moment a group of the king's soldiers appeared behind the friends. Being a strange man, the king had been unsettled by the calm contentment of Abdul. So he had said to the soldiers, 'Go after the three and kill the one who carries neither money nor wife.'

When Haroun saw the soldiers heading for him, he fled, and no one knows what happened to him.

Meanwhile, Anim, Abdul and the princess carried on their way. Eventually they reached a fast-flowing river.

'It's hard enough to get myself over here,' grumbled Anim. 'Here – you help her.'

So saying, he pushed the princess towards Abdul.

The heavy sack anchored Abdul safely as he crossed the river, and he held firmly onto the princess's hand. Anim was not so lucky. The current swept him away and he was never seen again.

Later, as Abdul and the princess ate a splendid meal in a pleasant village, he smiled at her.

'You know, my dear,' he said, 'there's a lot to be said for being content.'

(A very free adaptation of an old Iranian folk tale.)

Information for the teacher

1 Middle Eastern folk tales are a rich seam of material for assemblies. Whilst many involve fantastic happenings, princes and princesses, the significance of Allah is often apparent.

2 A Biblical quotation which is appropriate for this story is: 'Happy is the man who has God as his helper, whose hope is in God.' (Psalm 146, 5)

3 A possible calendar link for this story is with St George's Day on 23rd April. The legendary St George, confident in his Christian faith, captured the child-eating dragon outside the Middle Eastern town of Sylene. He then took the captive beast into the town saying that he would kill it if the king would be baptised. The king, and fifteen thousand of the town's people, thus became baptised.

Hymn suggestion

Come and Praise Vol 2 'God in his love' No 76

Prayer

Dear God,
Teach us the value of contentment and give us the strength to resist feelings of envy, dissatisfaction, discontent, greed and jealousy.
  Help us to be people whose company others enjoy. Amen.

National Curriculum Cross Curricular Reference

This story is an excellent vehicle for drama. Indeed, this whole assembly could be produced in dramatic form. Its location could stimulate some geographical work in finding out more about Iran – its position, climate, products, people, etc.

6 How did they do it?

Introduction

How do they do it? Why did it happen? There are sometimes questions which nobody can answer, because there are still a lot of mysteries in the world. Today's story is the sort of mystery we all like – one which has a very happy ending.

Story

'Isn't it fantastic?' said Peter.
  'It certainly is,' replied Elizabeth. 'I wonder what England will be like?'
  'Well, we'll soon find out.'
  The two children, son and daughter of Professor Hunter, were leaving their home in Canada and going on a visit to England with their parents.
  'There's only one snag, though,' said Elizabeth.
  'What's that?'
  'Well, I don't like leaving our pets all that time.'
  As if they could understand, the pets looked up from the carpet where they were all lying comfortably. 'They' were Luath, a beautiful

golden Labrador retriever; Badger, a bull terrier who was now old and partly blind, and Tao, a sleek and comfort-loving Siamese cat.

'Oh, don't worry,' went on Peter. 'Dad's going to take them all to Uncle John's, so they'll be well looked after while we're away.'

So the arrangements went ahead. Professor Hunter took the three pets to the home of John Longbridge in his car. This was a day's journey because the two homes were three hundred miles apart, through some of Northern Canada's most wild and bitter countryside. On his return, the family left for England.

What happened next will always remain something of a mystery. Although the animals were being well looked after by Mr Longbridge, they must have become homesick for their own house and family. One morning, when he got up, they had all disappeared.

So began a fantastic journey. Through some of the loneliest, most difficult countryside in the world, the two dogs and the cat began a three-hundred-mile trek to retrace an unknown route.

We know that Tao was once nearly drowned and separated from her companions for three days, yet she caught up with them again. All survived dense wooded wilderness and raging rivers and streams. Finally, thin, exhausted and desperately hungry, they arrived home just hours after the Hunter family had got back from England.

Information for the teacher

1 The details of this story, such as they are, were researched and written about by Sheila Burnford in her book *The Incredible Journey*.

2 A calendar link could be made with another unusual journey which took place in April: on 12th April 1961 Yuri Gagarin made his 30,000 km/h (18,000 mph), 89-minute trip round the globe in his spacecraft *Vostok 1*. Other April links: Richard Trevithick, who died on 22nd April 1833, drove his first steam carriage in London in 1802 – this was one of the forerunners of the locomotive and heralded a great development in transport; John Metcalf, a blind man who died on 26th April 1810, earned his living at one time as a stage-coach driver!

3 If the aspect of the story concerning the loyalty and faithfulness of animals is to be developed further, an impressive link is with the story of Greyfriars Bobby. For fourteen years, Bobby, a Skye terrier, guarded the grave of his master Mr Gray, who died in Edinburgh. So famous became the little dog that, on his death, his collar and dinner bowl became exhibits in the Huntly Museum,

Edinburgh. *Greyfriars Bobby* is the title of a book telling his story (by Lavinia Derwent, published in Puffin).

For other amazing animal stories, the *Guinness Book of Pet Records*, edited by Gerald Wood, is a good source.

Hymn suggestion

Come and Praise Vol 2 'All the animals' No 80

Prayer

Let us think this morning about the qualities, the courage, and the loyalty of so many animals.

Let us learn from them, appreciate them, and make sure that if animals are ever in our care we treat them with respect, care, kindness and consideration.

National Curriculum Cross Curricular Reference

A closer look at the countryside and climate of northern Canada would be a geographical link. There is scope for some unusual dramatic activity. Science could be involved in studying the needs, diet, durability and strength of animals such as dogs and cats.

7 *Milkman extraordinary*

Introduction

Every day we see people we know and take for granted – until they do something special.

Story

Michael Buckley was happy. It was a brisk April day and he had just completed his milk round. As he drove his empty milk float through the streets of Tylerstown in Mid Glamorgan in Wales, he had nothing more serious on his mind than a nice cup of tea.

'Soon be home now,' he thought to himself as he turned the float into a long street.

'But . . . what's that? It can't be . . . ' Michael gasped as he happened to glance up at one of the houses he was passing. A second glance, however, confirmed his worst fears. Standing on a bedroom windowsill was a tiny child.

Trying not to frighten her, Michael stopped his milk float as quietly as he could.

'Don't worry, pet, you'll be all right,' he called, as he tried to walk as casually and unconcernedly as he could to the front door of the child's house. Once there, he gave a short rap on the door – all the while keeping his eye on the child, who was now obviously frightened and teetering backwards and forwards on the ledge.

'Come on, come on, hurry up,' muttered Michael as he hammered again on the door. Still nobody answered and as he looked up the milkman suddenly saw the little girl lose her balance completely.

Things then happened with a rush. With a cry of fear, the little girl began to fall towards the concrete path beneath her. Leaping away from the front door, Michael dashed in the falling child's direction and flung himself in a full-length dive. He caught her inches above the concrete.

The story had a completely happy ending. Despite Michael's efforts, fourteen-month-old Cerys Shirley did hit her head on the concrete and had to be taken to hospital. However, she was only bruised, and William Shirley, her father, had some nice things to say about her rescuer.

'We can't thank Mike enough,' said Mr Shirley. 'His quick thinking certainly saved Cerys's life. She had climbed over some toys and somehow got out onto the windowsill.'

'Anybody would have done the same as I did,' said the modest milkman.

Information for the teacher

1   This story happened in April 1990 and Michael Buckley attributed his life-saving dive to the fact that he had played a lot of rugby in his younger days. He was forty when this incident happened.
2   It is a useful exercise to ask the children, after an assembly like this, to find items in newspapers about the heroic actions of 'ordinary' people. Local newspapers are very valuable in this context. In this way a very useful file of assembly stories can be built up.

Come and Praise Vol 1 'Cross over the road' No 70

Prayer

Let us give thanks this morning for those 'ordinary' people whose courage, quick thinking and speed of action is so often 'extraordinary'.

National Curriculum Cross Curricular Reference

There is a useful twin link here with both Science and Physical Education. In considering the advantages of keeping fit, Science could look at good habits in eating and exercise; Physical Education could be used to discover improved agility, speed of movement, etc.

Drama is a useful link with this story; finding and selecting other similar tales would be a useful exercise in reading and in discussing and assessing appropriate material.

8   *I don't like you*

Introduction

All of us like some people more than we do others. It's a strange thing, though, that when we really get to know somebody who we thought we didn't like, they usually seem much nicer!

Story

The mouse did not like the crow.

'I don't like you,' he used to say to himself, when he saw the black shape of the crow flying overhead in the sky. He was always very careful not to let the crow see him – after all, he didn't want to be the bird's dinner!

One day the mouse was scurrying about his business as usual when he heard a terrible noise. It was as if a thousand birds were all shouting at the same time. Heading for where the noise came from, the mouse came upon a terrible sight.

A huge net lay on the ground, and trapped inside it was a complete flock of doves. The mouse was horrified, and didn't hesitate for a minute.

'I'm coming!' he shouted, and scuffed up to the net as quickly as he could. 'No hunter is going to get you, my friends – not if I can help it.'

At once he began to gnaw the net with his small sharp teeth. His jaws ached and his body trembled with the effort, but slowly and surely he began to work through the net. Finally, with a sharp twang, it parted and the relieved doves swept away upwards to the sky. Their leader paused.

'Thank you, my friend,' he said. 'Thank you.'

High above, the crow had watched all that had taken place.

'That mouse,' he said to himself, 'is really some fellow. I'd like to be his friend.'

Later that day, the crow swooped down and perched outside the mouse's hole.

'Mouse!' he called out. 'That was a great deed you did today. I saw you rescue all those doves. I'd like us to be friends.'

Inside his hole the mouse was tired out. He'd been asleep until the crow's voice had wakened him.

'I don't like you,' he thought, as he listened to what the crow had to say. 'I'm sure this is a trick and if I go up there he'll eat me.'

So, no matter what the crow said, the mouse didn't answer. Finally the crow got tired of talking to himself.

'Are you still asleep in there, mouse? I know you must be tired after your rescue. I'll come back tomorrow and talk to you again.'

So saying, the crow flew off.

Next day the crow came again, and the day after, and the day after. Eventually the mouse could stand it no longer.

'Such nice things he says,' thought the mouse. 'Perhaps he really does want to be my friend.'

Cautiously he poked his nose out of his hole.

'Mouse!' cried the crow. 'How delighted I am to see you. We have so much to talk about.'

And so the mouse and the crow became the very best of friends. Sometime afterwards, there was a terrible shortage of water near their homes, and the crow carried his little friend to another place where there was plenty. Here they lived very happily.

Information for the teacher

1 This story is an adaptation of one of the many tales in the *Panchatantra*. This book of Indian stories, supposedly told by the great storyteller Pandit Vishnu Sharma, is a very useful source of assembly material.

2 As one of the main protagonists in this story is a crow, there is a useful, and unusual, calendar reference which could be used here. John Andubon was born on 26th April 1785. As a boy in Paris he

became an avid drawer of birds. Later as a businessman, he went to the United States, where he kept up this hobby. The end result was four volumes of hand-coloured drawings of all the known species of birds in North America: *The Birds of North America*.

3　For those who would like a different kind of calendar link, the second half of April is unusually rich in literary associations with 'storytellers'. It is thought that Shakespeare was born on the 23rd in 1564. Daniel Defoe (author of *Robinson Crusoe*) died on the 24th in 1731, and Charlotte Brontë was born on the 21st in 1816.

Hymn suggestion

Come and Praise Vol 1 'The Family of Man' No 69

Prayer

Dear God,
Help us to be more sensible and caring people. Teach us that it is so much better to say to ourselves, 'I'd like to get to know you better,' than 'I don't like you,' when we meet others.

Guide us too in our own behaviour so that others feel we can always be trusted and relied on. Amen.

National Curriculum Cross Curricular Reference

The telling of very simple stories 'with a message' is something which can be developed in English – both in reading and writing.

A geographical link could be the locating of India and some of its main features – towns, climate, terrain, etc. This could also provide an opportunity to listen to some Indian music.

9　Crane rescue

Introduction

When there is an accident, so often one ordinary person shows courage and quick-thinking more than anybody else. This morning's story tells us about such a person.

Story

The noise in the steel works was tremendous. Molten steel glowed with brilliant heat, hammers pounded, cranes lifted huge loads and men moved like ants amid the noise, heat and machinery.

High above the ground, in his electrically driven crane, driver William Hird looked down on his fellow workers.

'Glad I'm up here,' he thought. 'Being a crane driver is a really good job in this steel works. Well, better get in position again.'

William's hand moved to the controls of his crane. Suddenly, there was a shower of sparks from two of the electric cables, and within seconds the cabin was on fire.

'Help!' yelled William. 'Help! Fire!'

Down below, nobody saw or heard anything. The noise was too great and everybody was too busy to look up.

High above, however, in another crane cabin, Bernard Fisher happened to look down and immediately saw flames leaping from William's machine.

Without a moment's hesitation, Bernard brought his crane to a halt and clambered out. Balancing carefully, he climbed a ladder to the crane truck which ran high above the busy works floor. Then, going as fast as he could, he crossed the eighty-feet width of the gantry, and slipped down the ladder into the blazing cabin where William was still seated.

'OK, Bill, I'm on my way,' shouted Bernard, but William didn't move.

'Bill . . . Bill . . . are you OK?' shouted Bernard again as he reached the other driver and shook his shoulder. William fell against him. He had been overcome by the smoke and was now unconscious.

Bernard kicked open a trapdoor in the side of the crane cabin and dragged his unconscious friend through it. Then, with the other man's dead weight on his back, Bernard slowly inched his way up another twelve-foot-long ladder to a platform – and safety.

Down below, others had seen the crisis and help was on its way. The fire was soon put out, and William was rushed to hospital.

The story had a very happy ending. William made a complete recovery, and Bernard was a hero. All the papers told of his courage, quick-thinking and total disregard for his own safety. His colleagues in the steel works all clubbed together and bought him a gold watch and chain, and he was invited to Buckingham Palace where he was presented with a medal.

Information for the teacher

1   This incident took place in a Sheffield steel works on 26th April 1939. The medal awarded to Bernard Fisher was the Edward Medal. (This award, given for bravery, was superseded by the George Cross in 1940.) He received his medal from King George VI on 6th February 1940 and the citation declared that his action was 'carried out at great risk to himself and [that he] showed intelligence and initiative, [and] almost certainly saved Hird's life.'

2   This is another story which would fit in with the Biblical theme of 'not being discouraged by insurmountable difficulties'. (Judges 6, 8)

   An appropriate quotation from the Bible might be: 'in dealing with men it is God's purpose to test them and to see what they truly are . . .' (Ecclesiastes 3, 18)

3   Useful addresses are: Royal Society for the Prevention of Accidents, Cannon House, The Priory, Queensway, Birmingham B4 6BS; British Steel Corporation, 12 Addiscombe Road, Croydon CR9 3JH.

Hymn suggestion

Come and Praise Vol 1 'He who would valiant be' No 44

Prayer

Let us think this morning about the fact that every minute of every day, somebody, somewhere in the world, is helping another person. Let us give thanks for this, whether it is helping a blind person cross the road or saving a life as Bernard Fisher did.

National Curriculum Cross Curricular Reference

'Factories' is a theme which could embrace Science and Technology. It could also include Music and/or poetry in getting the children to improvise music or write poetry which conveys the hustle, bustle and noise of the factory floor.

May

10   *The move*

Introduction

Think for a minute about your bedroom. Are any of your favourite toys in it? Have you got a special bedspread? Is yours a comfortable bed? Now listen to this morning's story.

Story

Jessica could remember when Mum and Dad first talked about it.

'We'll certainly be better off there,' Dad had said. 'There are more rooms for the kids, the garden's bigger and I can get to work in half the time.'

'I don't know, Jack,' Mum had said doubtfully. 'We're so settled here.'

'It'll be all right, you'll see,' Dad went on. 'I think — Harry, stop moving that food about.'

Harry was Jessica's eighteen-month-old brother who was far too young to know what anybody was talking about. But Jessica kept hearing Mum and Dad talking about this 'moving'. And then one day it really happened.

'Well, we're moving on Wednesday,' said Mum. 'After school on Monday you'd better start packing the things in your bedroom.'

'Mum,' said Jessica in a small voice, 'I don't want to move. I like it here.'

'Our new house is really nice,' answered Mum with a smile. 'You'll like it there even more.'

Jessica was miserable at school. She kept thinking of her bedroom – all her toys in their special places, her warm, comfortable bed with the Snoopy bedspread, the window where she could look out at next door's cat sneaking across the lawn. She didn't want to move!

Wednesday came all too soon. Mum had arranged for Jessica to have the day off school and when she woke and looked at the packed crates and curtainless window she felt more miserable than ever. The removal men arrived and everything was soon in a frenzy. Men with boxes clattered up and down stairs, the cat hid in the meter cupboard, Mum and Dad were tetchy – only Harry seemed to enjoy it.

Finally the house was empty and the family got into their car and set off, following the removal van. When they reached the new house, the dashing about started all over again. While Jessica was standing miserably holding Harry's hand Mum had a quiet word with Dad.

'Jack, I'm going to get Jessica's room ready first to try and cheer her up. Why don't you drive back to the old house and make sure we haven't left anything? Take Jessica with you. My mother's coming over to look after Harry.'

'Good idea,' said Dad. 'Come on, Jessica,' he called.

Soon the two of them were making the trip back to the old house. As they turned into the familiar street Jessica felt tears prick her eyes. This was home and it always would be – why did they have to move? Soon they were parked and Dad was stomping through the house. While he did so, Jessica went up to her old room. It looked so cold and bare and even . . . unfriendly. She felt confused – she didn't seem to belong here any more.

Dad found a couple of books they'd overlooked and soon they were back in the car again. The new street had a couple of nice trees in it and when they reached their new house Mum was waving out of an upstairs window.

'Jessica – I've got your room ready. Come on up and have a look!'

Dutifully Jessica plodded up the stairs. How could it ever be as good as her old bedroom – just how *could* it? Mum stepped aside and Jessica went in.

There were her toys lined up just like they'd always been. Snoopy grinned up from the bed and everything seemed a bit bigger. Some new flowered curtains blew in a cool breeze from the open window. It looked . . . well . . . it looked . . . nice . . . really very . . .

'Jessica!' Dad's voice sounded from downstairs. 'There's somebody here to see you.'

When Jessica got downstairs again, a girl of about her own age, with the brightest ginger hair she had ever seen, was standing next to Dad.

'Hi,' said the girl. 'My name's Natasha and I live next door. I thought you might like to come round while your Mum and Dad are sorting the house out.'

'Oh . . . thanks,' murmured Jessica.

'Come on, then,' said Natasha cheerfully. 'Moving's rotten, isn't it? But this is a great place to live, you know. There's a smashing stream, and woods just a couple of minutes away. And Floella lives just two doors away and . . .'

As Natasha chattered away, Jessica felt a smile creepiing over her face. It was going to be all right here. Yes, there was no doubt about it – it was going to be all right.

Information for the teacher

1 The themes of changes, uncertainty, welcomes, etc, could be discussed before the assembly, or developed in post-assembly discussions. If appropriate, one or two children could speak of their personal experiences during the assembly presentation, after the story.
2 A bit of thought and preparation could go into music to accompany this assembly. 'Home' is a powerful theme in popular music – 'Keep the home fires burning', 'Show me the way to go home', 'Pasadena', 'Home on the Range', etc.
3 The following is a famous quotation from a child of refugee parents: 'Yes we have a home, but no house to put round it.'
4 An unusual, and stimulating, calendar reference could be with 5th May. It was on this date in 1944 that tools used by men of the Old Stone Age (250,000 years ago) were discovered forty miles from Nairobi in Kenya.

Hymn suggestion

Come and Praise Vol 1 'O Lord, all the world belongs to you' No 39

Prayer

Dear God,
Let us give thanks for our homes and all who make them so precious to us. Let us pray too for those unfortunate people who have no home. Please give them hope for the future. Amen.

National Curriculum Cross Curricular Reference

History and Geography would be closely linked in a study of homes in different parts of the world, and their development. The Bible is a useful source of information on early homes and children are usually interested to know that early homes in Bible lands were literally 'houses of hair' – they were tents of weather-resistant textiles woven on looms.

Both drama and discussion could be linked with English in depicting and describing homes. Technology could be involved in considering machines in the home, how the water system works, etc. Music could be considerably involved: see point 2 above, under *Information for the teacher*.

11   *It's not fair*

Introduction

None of us can do anything about how we look – we were just born this way! Sometimes, though, the way a person or creature looks or moves makes others dislike him of her. How unfair this is. Many people feel this way about spiders, but old stories show them in a very different light.

Story

There are a lot of spiders around – in Britain alone there are many more than two hundred thousand billion of them! Although lots of people say they are frightened of spiders, there are some old stories about them which are very interesting.

For instance, it was said that, at the first Christmas when Jesus was born in the stable, one of the first creatures to appear was a spider. Lowering itself down from the roof, it began busily to spin a web over the manger containing the newborn baby. This was to protect him.

There is another spider story about the birth of Jesus: when King Herod ordered his soldiers to kill all newborn baby boys because of his fear of the 'new King', Joseph and Mary took Jesus and fled before the soldiers could find them. On their journey they stopped one night and hid in a cave. While they slept, a party of soldiers reached the cave and were about to look inside when they saw that a spider's web completely covered the entrance.

'Waste of time looking in there,' they said to each other. 'Nobody can have gone in there recently, not with that spider's web over the entrance.'

Then there is the story of Robert I, known as Robert the Bruce, who was crowned King of Scotland in 1306. At this time his country was full of English invaders and in trying to drive them out his army lost a great battle and he had to flee for his life.

Hiding out on Rathlin Island, he watched a spider spinning its web. Time and time again it ran into difficulties and time and time again it started again and would not give up.

'What a marvellous example,' said Robert to himself. 'We should be like the spider and learn how important it is to keep on trying at whatever we are doing.' Robert got his army together again and led them in successfully driving the English out of Scotland.

Information for the teacher

1 Probably the most famous spider legend concerns Athena and Arachne. Arachne was a Greek girl who was so good at weaving that she challenged the goddess Athena to see who could produce the best piece of work. Arachne duly won, but Athena was so angry that she tore up Arachne's work and turned the girl into a spider.

2 Anansi, or 'Mr Spider', the great trickster of West African origin and fame, was originally thought to have created the world. There are dozens of stories about him and his popularity is now worldwide.

3 There are several Biblical quotations which could be used in connection with this material:

> Countless Kings are made by your hand,
> And the earth is full of your creatures.
> (Psalm 104)

> Do not overrate one man for his good looks or be repelled by
>   another man's appearance.
> The bee is small among the winged creatures,
> Yet her perfume takes first place for sweetness.
> (Ecclesiasticus 11, 2–3)

> As opportunity offers, let us work for the good of all.
> (Galatians 6, 9–10)

4 A possible calendar link for this material is 3rd May. On this date Columbus 'discovered' Jamaica – one of the areas where Anansi has become most famous.

Hymn suggestion

Come and Praise Vol 1 'All creatures of our God and King' No 7

Prayer

Let us think this morning of all the many living creatures in the world. Let us learn not to judge them, or human beings, by their appearance.

Let us always remember the needs of those creatures who are our pets, and care for them with love and attention.

National Curriculum Cross Curricular Reference

The most obvious link with this material is with Science, and considerable extending work can be done here. The spider in folklore would yield some interesting work in English and/or History.

There are possibilities here for Music and movement. For instance, the fast 'Tarantella' dance originated from Taranto in the south east of Italy. Here people thought that a tarantula spider's bite would kill and the only antidote was to dance until exhausted.

12   James Merryweather

Introduction

Every town these days has its library, post office, police station – and its fire station. Although fire stations and fire brigades are very important, it took the efforts of one man, more than anybody else, to make others realise this. His name was James Merryweather.

Story

The warm May sunshine shone down on a miserable scene. A group of people in black clothes moved slowly and tearfully through a London cemetery in a long funeral procession.

Watching them, with his hat in his hand, stood a burly, determined-looking man.

'It need never have happened,' he said to the friend who stood beside him. 'In fact, it *should* never have happened. More people dead because their house burnt down when the fire could have been put out.'

'I know, James, but what can you do?' asked the friend.

'I'm going to form my own fire brigade, that's what I'm going to do,' replied James Merryweather.

It was 1862 and James, a skilled engineer, had been trying for years to get the London Fire Establishment to take an interest in his steam fire engine. Despite many fires, and many deaths, they still preferred to use the old method of pumping water by hand. James argued that this was slower and nothing like so effective.

Now, tired of having to help the authorities, he organised his own fire brigade.

'I want brave men,' he said to anybody who joined him, 'but they will have the best fire engines possible. They'll be able to get to fires quicker than anybody else and they'll be able to put them out much more rapidly.'

There was no shortage of volunteers and soon James's fire engines were a familiar sight as they raced round London dealing with various fire alarms. His reputation grew.

'Have you heard about James Merryweather's fire brigade?'

'Yes, he really gets things done.'

'Far better than anybody else.'

'Well, he's always thinking about new ideas and working them out, isn't he?'

Finally, in 1866, the authorities decided they miust do something better. The London Metropolitan Fire Brigade was formed and James's steam pumps were accepted everywhere and put into use.

'Great,' said James. 'Now we'll be able to put out fires more efficiently. But what we've also got to do is to try and make sure that they never start.'

So James became one of the first people to think seriously about fire precautions. He wanted experts to look over buildings before people moved in to live there, to make sure they were as safe as possible from fire risks. In 1897 he said that no theatre should ever be allowed to open until officers of the Fire Brigade had made sure it was safe.

While James was doing this, he was still building bigger and better fire engines, and writing the first book on proper fire-fighting methods.

'I don't know where you find the time to do it all,' said one of his friends.

'I must,' replied James. 'Don't you see how important it all is? If what I do can save only one life, it's worth it. Remember, it might be your life – or your son's or daughter's or mother's.'

So James carried on his ceaseless work and by the time he died he had invented more than two hundred and fifty improvements to fire-fighting equipment.

Information for the teacher

1   This is ideal material to fit into the theme of 'Those who help us', which often features in a series of assemblies.

2   There are some interesting May calendar associations to link with this story. For instance, it was as far back as 13th May 1680 that the first Fire Insurance Company began selling insurance.

Disastrous fires occurred on these dates: in New Jersey, USA, on 6th May 1937, when the airship *Hindenberg* caught fire after crossing the Atlantic: and on 11th May 1941, when London suffered its worst air raid, during which fourteen hundred people died and Westminster Abbey, St Paul's Cathedral and the British Museum were all damaged by fire.

The worst-ever number of casualties caused by a fire was in Japan in 1923 when sixty thousand died in a fire caused by an earthquake.

3   The first fire brigades were organised by the Romans. These were known as the corps of *Vigiles* (watchmen) and were created followiing a great fire in Rome in the year 6 AD.

4   In another context, 'fire' is often a theme linked with RE, particularly at this time of the year with the symbolic link between Whitsun and fire. Flowers appearing over the heads of Apostles in Christian art symbolised the presence of the Holy Ghost.

St Anthony of Padua is the patron saint of protection against fire.

5   Two useful addresses in this context are: Fire Protection Association, 140 Aldersgate Street, London EC1A 4HY, and the London Fire Brigade, 8 Albert Embankment, London SE1 7SD.

Hymn suggestion

Come and Praise Vol 1 'Water of life' No 2

Prayer

Let us give thanks this morning for those people whose skill, inventiveness, courage and determination do so much to help others. We pray that their advice and suggestions may be listened to for the good of us all. Amen.

National Curriculum Cross Curricular Reference

Fire – its causes, effects, prevention, etc, is a subject which can stimulate an enormous amount of work in Science and Technology. Geography could be involved in locating areas where great fires have taken place – London, Chicago, San Francisco, etc; and in an historical context the history of fire brigades is both interesting and informative.

This is a subject which often stimulates unusually good work from primary children in areas like Art and poetry.

There are also opportunities for creating improvised music and listening to music such as: Falla's *Ritual Fire Dance*; Stravinsky's *Firebird Suite*; and the many folk and popular songs related to the subject – 'Fire Down Below', 'Light up the Fires', etc.

13   Leading the way

Introduction

Imagine a whole lot of strange children suddenly appeared in the playground of your school when your class was out there. What do you think might happen? This morning's story is one to make us think about a situation like this.

Story

Muhammad was on his travels again. He had reached a town after a long journey through the desert, and he liked what he saw.

'This is a pleasant place,' he said to himself., 'There are plenty of cool trees and comfortable buildings, and everybody seems to be well enough. What a very nice place to live.'

Muhammad rested in the town for a few days. As usual, he talked to a lot of people and even in such a short time he became well known.

One morning, just before he was preparing to leave, there was a great commotion in the town.

'There's a whole lot of them!'

'They're coming in through the gates now.'

'Never seen anything like it.'

'Goodness knows what happened to them.'

Muhammad was swept along with the crowd of people who pushed through the town's narrow streets towards the entry gate. When they reached it they split into two groups, one on either side of the road. There they watched, silently, as a long crocodile of people wound its way out of the desert through the town's gate.

The line moved slowly because the people in it looked near to collapse. Bleached by the sun, what few clothes they wore hung in rags and tatters from their starved looking bodies. Many were bandaged, some helped weaker friends to stagger along and all had a dazed and beaten look.

Muhammad became more and more restless as the pitiful group staggered to a stop and stood with downcast eyes.

'I've heard about them,' said a man next to Muhammad. 'Their town was ransacked and they've been wandering in the desert for weeks.'

'That's what I heard, too,' said another man, staring at the group.

Muhammad could stand it no longer. He stepped in front of the townspeople.

'How much longer are you going to stand and stare?' he asked. 'When is somebody going to do something?'

Sheepishly most looked away, but not one man.

'Wait!' he cried, and hurried to his house nearby. Within seconds he was back with a pile of clothes over his arm and food and drink in both hands.

He hurried to the group of worn-out people and began to give these things to them. When his friends saw what he had done they moved hurriedly away – and returned equally quickly with more clothes, more food and drinks and even sums of money.

Muhammad watched all this quietly.

'It is as I thought,' he said to one of his friends. 'If one person sets a good example there will be plenty who will follow him.'

Information for the teacher

1 A useful calendar link for this story is 7th May. It was on this date in 1945 that the Second World War ended in Europe – and there is a modern counterpart of this tale which is very evocative. At a parade in Moscow, German prisoners of war were paraded through the streets. Many of them were in a pitiful condition. The watching crowds had themselves suffered innumerable hardships and privations, but as the line of men went by an old woman broke through the line of Soviet troops guarding the prisoners and gave a hunk of black bread to a wounded German soldier. Within seconds others in the crowd were pressing what little they had onto the desperate prisoners.

2 A Muslim is required to give two-and-a-half per cent of his income to the needy or poor. A concern for others is a fundamental tenet

of the religion. This is reflected in many of the sayings of Muhammad, which are collected in a book called *Treasure* by Waheed-ud-Din, obtainable from Islamic Publications, London Mosque, 16 Gressenhall Road, London SW18.

Hymn suggestion

Come and Praise Vol 2 'God in his love' No 76

Prayer

This morning let us listen to the words of a Muslim proverb and then spend half a minute thinking quietly about them. The words are: 'He is best loved who does most good to others.'

National Curriculum Cross Curricular Reference

Geography and Science could be linked in considering the climate of the Middle East where Islam began. (Mecca is in Saudi Arabia.)

Science could also be involved in studying the effects of fasting (with reference to Ramadan, the month of fasting when Muslims eat nothing between sunrise and sunset).

The story provides plenty of discussion material on subjects like embarrassment, showing initiative, taking the lead, giving freely, etc. It also has strong dramatic possibilities.

14   *Enough is enough*

Introduction

Perhaps you complain when you are told it is bedtime. Perhaps you want a little extra cake when Mum says you have had enough. It is tempting to want a little more, but this is sometimes not fair on the people we share our lives with.

This morning's story is about a man who had great good fortune – but still wanted a little more . . . and a little more . . .

Story

The moon shone down on the icy, snow-covered countryside.

Suddenly, through the still night air, came the jolly sound of a fiddle being played. There, skating across the iced-up river, was Janek. Janek was a herdsman who loved playing the fiddle. He had been playing at a party and was going home.

Reaching the other side of the river, he set off homewards, and was just about to pass a small hill when, to his absolute astonishment, a door in the hill opened and a beautiful lady stepped out.

Janek thought he was seeing a ghost and was about to run away when she spoke.

'Don't be afraid,' called out the lady. 'Your music was so lovely I just had to find out where it came from.'

Janek stood as if rooted to the spot as the lady told him her story.

Long ago she had been a queen of Poland and every night between eleven o'clock and midnight she was allowed to come back to the land she loved.

'Now,' she went on, 'play a tune for me. If there is anything you ever want you can find me here at the hour I have mentioned.'

With trembling fingers Janek played once again. As he finished, a distant clock began striking midnight and the queen disappeared into the hillside again.

Now, Janek was a wonderful fiddler but he was not so good as a herdsman. He spent a lot of time daydreaming. One day he lost one of his farmer's cows. His master was furious. The cow couldn't be found and Janek was told he must pay for it. He had no money and was desperately thinking what he might do, when – he remembered the mysterious queen.

That night he went back to the hillside and played a tune. Immediately the secret door opened and the queen appeared.

'Welcome, Janek,' she said. 'Please play for me.'

Janek did this, and then told her his troubles.

'You may go into my hill,' said the queen, 'but take only the ten gold pieces you need to pay for the lost cow.'

Janek went into the hill and gasped. There at the bottom of a flight of steps, and lit by flickering light, was a fabulous hoard of treasure. Remembering what the queen had said, the fiddler took only ten pieces of gold and returned to the outside of the hill.

Another night, Janek came back to ask the queen for help again. He wanted to marry a young woman called Margaret, but Margaret did not love him. The queen told him about the touch of a secret fork which would make Margaret love him. Now all seemed well, until Margaret's father refused to let his daughter marry Janek because he was such a poor man.

So Janek returned to the secret hillside once again.

'Play for me, Janek,' said the queen, and when he had finished she listened to his latest story.

'I know that I can be a good farmer,' said Janek. 'All I need is enough money to buy a piece of land which I know is for sale.'

'How much is it?' asked the queen.

'Four hundred gold pieces,' replied Janek.

'Very well,' said the queen. 'Go into the hill, down the steps and take only the four hundred pieces you need.'

'Thank you, thank you,' said Janek.

'But,' the queen went on, 'remember it is nearly midnight and when the clock strikes, the door will disappear and if you are still inside you will be trapped in the hill.'

'Oh, I'll be quick and only take exactly what I need,' said Janek. He hurried into the hill.

Hurriedly, he counted out the four hundred pieces and then, as he was going back up the stairs, he saw them. Standing on the floor in a corner was a magnificent pair of bright red boots. Janek stopped.

'It can't do any harm to try them,' he thought to himself. Putting down his gold, Janek slid on the boots. They were a perfect fit! The soft leather warmed his ankles and he looked to where he had lain his own tattered old boots.

'If only . . . ' he thought. Then, in the distance, he heard the clock begin to strike midnight. Desperately, he seized the gold, raced up the steps and flung himself through the hillside door before he was trapped.

'Safe!' he gasped as he burst out into the night air. Then he remembered the queen's words, 'Take only what you need.'

No sooner had these words come into his head than – his feet were burning! Tearing at the boots with his hands, Janek tried again and again to pull them off. All the time the heat grew hotter and hotter . . .

The next morning, passing travellers saw something lying by the roadside. What had obviously been a good pair of boots lay smouldering on the grass, the smoke still rising. As for Janek – he was never ever seen again.

Information for the teacher

1   This is an assembly which could be presented with a judicious mixture of readings and mime.

2   There are possibilities for linking it with the Bible story centred on

the saying: 'It is easier for a camel to go through the eye of a needle than for a rich man to enter the Kingdom of God.' This story of man's desire for riches on earth can be found in Luke 18, 18–26.

3 A possible calendar link here is with 9th May 1671, the date on which Colonel Blood stole the Crown Jewels from the Tower of London. Alternatively, 23rd May 1701 was the date on which Captain Kidd, the infamous pirate, was hanged.

Hymn suggestion

Come and Praise Vol 1 'The best gift' No 59

Prayer

Let us think this morning about sharing the good things of our lives and being thankful for what we have. Let us remember that to want more is often to get less.

National Curriculum Cross Curricular Reference

There are obvious links with Music here – listening to some violin music, examining a violin, doing some practical work with a tightened string over hollow boxes. The theme of 'sound' could be carried over into Science. The history of musical instruments, and in particular the violin, would be a useful exercise. This would also incorporate Geography, in particular Mittenwald (the German town famous for its violin-making) and Poland, the location of the story.

15 *Christian Aid week*

Introduction

Every May there is a week when we think about Christian aid to people all over the world who are less fortunate than we are, and need as much help as they can be given.

Story

This morning we are going to hear about two of the sort of people who are given help by the Christian Aid organisation. Listening to their stories makes us think about the many things we take for granted.

First of all, let's think about water. How much do we use each day – to wash ourselves, drink, use to flush the toilet, and so on. Whenever we need it, whatever we need it for, it always seems to be there.

This is not the case for a lady called Tazunda who lives in a wooden hut in a tiny village in Africa. This is a very dry part of the world and the nearest water for Tazunda comes from a muddy hole which is ten minutes' walk away from her hut.

Twice every morning and twice every afternoon, Tazunda walks barefoot from her hut to this water hole. When she gets there she has to scoop water from the dirty iron drum sunk into the water hole. She does this with a jug and pours the water into a rusty old 23-litre bucket. Then she carries the jug and the bucket back home.

Every single day Tazunda must do this. This water must do for her family of four and the amount she gets every day is only the same amount as we use when we flush the toilet twice.

Sanja is much younger than Tazunda and she lives in Nepal, in the shadow of Mount Everest and the other great Himalayan mountains. Sanja was born with a disease called polio and for the first ten years of her life she could only crawl. At first this wasn't too bad because her mother could carry her, but when she was ten years old and her mother had to go to market Sanja could only crawl round behind her in the dirt, dust, noise and bustle. Nobody thought that she would ever be able to walk.

One day, however, a worker from the Save the Children organisation saw Sanja crawling round in the market. Soon help was being offered to her and her mother. Sanja was taken to a health centre in a village called Chautara and after a year's exercises on parallel bars, and with the help of crutches, she has learned to walk.
(These stories were adapted from Save The Children information.)

Information for the teacher

1   Most primary schools are circulated with information, photographs and very helpful assembly material by the Christian Aid Organisation for their week in early May. If you do not receive this information, the organisation's address is: Christian Aid, PO Box No 1, London SW9 8BH. There are also local secretaries to contact who are usually most helpful.

Save the Children is another organisation which does an excellent job, and it also provides first-class material for schools. A useful contact is with the Education Unit, Save the Children Fund,

Mary Datchelor House, 17 Grove Lane, London SE5 8RD.

2   Tazunda comes from Western Zimbabwe. In Africa as a whole, thirty to fifty per cent of child deaths under five are caused by contaminated water.

3   To illustrate that concern for others is a feeling which pervades all religions, two quotations might be useful:

> He who does not help to turn the rolling wheels of this great world lives a lost life. (Hindu)

> A man should treat everybody and everything in the world as he himself would like to be treated. (Jain)

4   For information on water provision in the UK, to make comparisons with Third World problems, contacts with local Water Board Authorities could be useful.

Hymn suggestion

Come and Praise Vol 2 'Water of Life' No 2

Prayer

Let us think this morning of all those people, all over the world, whose lives are desperately hard and who are often suffering terribly.

Let us give thanks to the workers everywhere who are helping, and let us pray that the kindness of others will continue to raise money to support the work that is being done to help.

National Curriculum Cross Curricular Reference

A tremendous amount of work can be done in Science, concentrating simply on water for human needs. This can be expanded to consider what else is needed for good health, how climate and privations can cause bad health, medical needs, and so on.

There is much scope for discussion, and in this context some words by Perez de Cuellar, Secretary General of the United Nations in 1987, could be a starting point: 'The way a society treats its children reflects its qualities of compassion and protective caring.'

The material distributed by the Christian Aid organisation for Christian Aid Week often contains much geographical information and this could be used to explore wider problems – climate, lack of local resources, distance from Western help, communication difficulties, etc.

Some Technology could be involved in considering and creating water containers.

16   The grave

Introduction

Have you ever noticed how much attention we pay to the way other people behave? Listen to this morning's story . . .

Story

'I am going to travel and see something of the world,' Abdul said to himself.

So he set off, with his donkey as his only companion. For twelve years he travelled through deserts and mountains, staying in many different places and meeting many different people. He became a much wiser man.

One day he was travelling through the mountains of Kashmir.

'This is one of the most difficult trips yet,' Abdul muttered to his faithful donkey as they toiled higher and higher up into the thin air.

'Come on my . . .' Abdul stopped speaking. His donkey was suddenly slowing down. 'What is . . .'

This time, before Abdul could finish what he was going to say, the donkey slipped quietly to the ground, and there it died. It had finally become exhausted with old age and ceaseless travel.

Abdul was heartbroken. In all the years of his journeys the donkey had been his faithful companion and friend. Now he was dead.

After a while, the traveller looked up from his tears. Seeing the beautiful scenery around him he found he had lost his desire to travel further.

'This will be my home,' he said aloud.

He set about burying the donkey and, when he had done so, he marked the grave with a simple mound of earth. Then he began making a home for himself nearby.

As the days and weeks went by, he made sure that the donkey's grave was always beautifully looked after.

Now, the path Abdul had been following was a busy one and many travellers passed by there. They noticed the grave, and the man who cared for it so lovingly, and they talked about this.

'That must have been a dear friend who lies buried there.'

'How carefully that man cares for the grave.'

'I think it must belong to somebody who was really important.'

So the tales went on. Abdul said nothing. One day a very rich man came by. He had heard all the stories about the man who lived on the mountain.

'Now sir,' he said to Abdul, 'I've heard about the way you care for your lost friend. I'd like to help.'

So the rich man built a shrine over the donkey's grave. In order that there would always be money to keep it in good repair, he had terraces cut into the hillside, where the villagers could grow crops to sell. This helped the villagers grow more prosperous, and the whole community cared for each other.

One day Abdul stood on the hill beside the donkey's grave and looked at the happy village spread before him.

'Now my dear friend,' he said, 'look what a simple donkey has achieved.'

Information for the teacher

1   Although this is an adaptation of an old folk tale which has no link with Christianity, there are many Christian associations with donkeys.

   When St Anthony of Padua was seeking to convert a group of people he lost patience and said that it would be easier to make a wild donkey kneel down than it would be to persuade them to listen to him. At this point a nearby donkey knelt, the unbelievers listened and were converted to Christianity.

   St Jerome's monastery was built thanks to the donkey who carried all the wood.

   The donkey also features in Nativity scenes ('the ox and the ass') and in Jesus's entry into Jerusalem.

2   In times gone by in the Middle East, and elsewhere, the ass was of enormous importance to its owner. It ate only a quarter of the barley which a horse ate, it was particularly sure-footed in seeking out desert paths, and it could be used for hauling and ploughing.

3   One possible calendar link could be with 8th May. This was the day, in 1828, on which the Swiss philanthropist Jean Henri Dunant was born. As a traveller he was an eyewitness to the terrible battle of Solferino on 24th June 1859. He was appalled at the high number of casualties – forty thousand – and organised emergency help for French and Austrian wounded alike. He ultimately

founded the International Red Cross and was the first to be awarded the Nobel Peace Prize, in 1901. (He shared the award with Frédéric Passy.)

Hymn suggestion

Come and Praise Vol 1 'Travel on' No 42

Prayer

Let us think this morning about some words Jesus said: 'If you want to be a leader you must be a servant.'

Let us pray that we may have the strength to behave in a way which is both a help and an example to other people. Amen.

National Curriculum Cross Curricular Reference

Locating Kashmir and finding something out about it would be a useful geographical exercise. Science could be involved in finding out more about donkeys – their life-spans, habits, needs, etc. There are several discussion possibilities for English (what people need on journeys, etc), and some opportunities for some interesting work in Art.

17 Determination

Introduction

Somebody once said that it is not important what you have in life – it's what you do with what you have that counts. This morning's story begins on the M6 motorway.

Story

The thirty-eight-ton lorry was approaching a traffic queue on the motorway.

'Better start slowing down,' thought driver Stuart Braye, easing his foot onto the brake. To his horror, the lorry didn't slow down fast enough – his brakes had failed! Even though the lorry had slowed to only thirty miles an hour, the crash was a bad one. For thirty minutes Stuart was trapped in his cab, and then he was rushed to hospital for an emergency operation.

'You're lucky to be alive,' said the doctor when Stuart recovered consciousness. 'Very lucky – but I'm afraid we've had to remove one of your legs.'

Although he was shocked, Stuart felt so thankful to be alive that he made a quick recovery. Learning to walk again, however, was very difficult. It was six months before he could be fitted with an artificial leg, and then he had to have another operation.

Stuart used this time to study on a business course so that he could prepare himself for a more suitable job when he was better, but all the time he worried about how he would be able to run again.

'I've always liked running and been a bit of an athlete,' thought Stuart to himself, 'and I'm not going to give up now.'

So he started to learn to run again. It was very painful and so that no one could see how much he had to struggle he ran round the streets near his house in the darkness when everybody else was in bed. Agonisingly slowly, Stuart began to get better and better at running. He got an extension for his artificial leg, called a 'Flexifoot', from America, and this helped him enormously. He joined an athletic club and began to train seven days a week.

Gradually Stuart's determination began to pay off in several ways. He began to set up fast times in races and became a well-known member of the British Amputees Sports Association. His courage, determination and success also led to his being invited to give talks to doctors and to patients who had recently lost one or both of their legs.

Stuart Braye is the sort of man who doesn't know the meaning of 'giving up'.

'Don't call me disabled,' he says, 'just say I'm physically challenged!'

Information for the teacher

1   This story could be linked to several medical anniversaries in May. Florence Nightingale was born on 12th May 1820; Edward Jenner made the first successful smallpox vaccination on the 14th in 1796; the Royal Flying Doctor Service began in Australia on the 15th in 1928.

2   Useful addresses could include:

   Central Council for the Disabled, 25 Mortimer Street, London W1N 8AB. The Royal Association for Disability and Rehabilitation (RADAR) is at the same address.

   REACH (The Association for children with Artificial Arms), 11 Shelley Road, Old Marks, Cheltenham, Gloucestershire.

Hymn suggestion

Come and Praise Vol 1 'A man for all the people' No 27

Prayer

Let us think this morning about the example people like Stuart Braye set us. Let us pray that their courage and determination helps others who are in difficulty and distress. Amen.

National Curriculum Cross Curricular Reference

There is an obvious link here between Science, health and the human body. Technology could involve practical activities in considering how human joints work, and what is required in artificial substitutes. PE could also be involved in a practical consideration of which parts of the body move in order to perform various movements.

English writing possibilities exist in detailed, descriptive work of physical movements.

18 This month

Introduction

In May there is a real feeling that summer is coming and there are plenty of messages to tell us this.

This month

A man who spent his lifetime studying the English countryside said that it reached its most beautiful on 18th May every year. This man's name was W H Hudson and if we look around on this date we can certainly see what he means.

Let's start with trees. It is very strange that things as large as trees have very small flowers and seeds. By 18th May these flowers and seeds look their most beautiful. The hawthorn and horse chestnut are in blossom, the greenish-yellow flowers of the sycamore dangle in big clusters, and there are tiny white flowers on holly and catkins on oaks.

If you visit a wood, looking down is as exciting as looking up at this time of year. There is often a 'carpet' of blue, where masses of bluebells are growing. These contrast with the red of red campions. On roadsides leading to woods, cow parsley seems to grow taller almost by the minute and great heads of blossom appear on it. Watch out, too, for buttercups and forget-me-nots. White deadnettles take a bit more finding but it is worth having a search for them and then seeing if you agree with their old country name – 'white archangels'.

Of course, this is a time when everything grows – and that means some difficulties for people too. Along country lanes weeds and grass start to grow to a height which creates danger for traffic, and have to be cut down.

In the fields weeds start to grow as fast as the corn and the fields may have to be treated with sprays. These are often fitted to the back of tractors and they kill the weeds while letting the corn continue to grow.

In times gone by the dew on the grass in the early morning in May was thought to make girls and ladies more beautiful. So it was not unusual to see them 'washing their faces' in the grass.

People liked to enjoy themselves in May in other ways, too. There was dancing round the maypole on the first of the month and great celebrations on 29th May. This is 'Oak Apple Day' when King Charles II rode into London as the new king in 1660. Before this the Puritans had ruled and the reason people gave this day its name was because the king had hidden from the Puritan army in an oak tree after the Battle of Worcester.

So May is a month to take a deep breath and enjoy all that the countryside has to offer. An old rhyme reminds us of this:

> Here we come a-piping
> In Springtime and in May,
> Green fruit a-ripening,
> And winter fled away.

Information for the teacher

1 The word 'May' reportedly comes from Maia, mother of the god Mercury. The Anglo-Saxons had a more descriptive name for this month – 'Tri-Milchi', denoting the fact that the ideal grassy conditions meant that cattle could now be milked three times a day.

2 The Puritans denounced maypoles and maypole dancing (in 1644). On the restoration of the monarchy, Charles II reintroduced May Day in style by erecting an 134-foot-high maypole in the Strand.

3 The hawthorn has symbolic associations with the return of summer. Hung outside a cowshed, it was believed to guarantee good milk; placed in the rafters of a house, it was believed to

keep evil spirits away.

4   The start of growth begins with a mean daily temperature of
43°F (6°C).

Hymn suggestion

Come and Praise Vol 1 'For the beauty of the earth' No 11

Prayer

Dear God,
Thank you for the beauty of the month of May. Thank you for our
senses of sight, smell and hearing which help us to enjoy it so much.

We pray for your help to make sure that people do nothing to
destroy the beautiful flowers, trees, woods and fields which look so
lovely at this time of year. Amen.

National Curriculum Cross Curricular Reference

May is an ideal month for taking children out of doors. As well as the
scientific possibilities of investigating flowers, trees and other natural
things, the opportunity should not be lost of considering directions,
distances, etc. A direction-finding compass (and someone who knows
how to use it!) should accompany parties outdoors. A pedometer also
provides interest and information and the 'Littleped' (obtainable from
Pedometers International Ltd, Ashby Lodge, Daventry, Northants,
NN11 5LB) is ideal for primary use.

Poems and pictures are often evoked by the sights and sounds of the
month; and there is considerable scope for musical appreciation.
Music could incorporate a selection of songs relevant to fairs and
dances, such as 'The Floral Dance', 'Widecombe Fair', 'Strawberry
Fair' and 'Scarborough Fair'.

19   Getting what you deserve

Introduction

People sometimes try to get things for themselves by being sly and
deceitful. This morning's story is a warning about the results of such
behaviour.

Story

Up on the hillside the wolf looked down on the flock of sheep. As the evening wind ruffled his coarse coat, he thought to himself, 'I'm so hungry, and there's nothing I'd like more for supper than one of those sheep down there.'

As he thought this, his eyes flicked to the burly figure of the shepherd who was guarding the sheep. He looked alert and fast-moving enough to see and deal with any approaching wolf. But the wolf had an idea. Lying nearby was an old sheepskin.

'If I were to disguise myself in this sheepskin and then mingle with the flock,' he thought, 'I could bide my time and then kill the fattest sheep for my supper. The shepherd would never even know I was there.'

Slipping into the sheepskin, the wolf found that it covered him perfectly. He approached the flock stealthily, and in no time at all he was among them. Not only did the shepherd not see him arrive, but the other sheep paid no attention to him either. Pretending to munch grass like the sheep, the wolf smiled to himself.

'So far so good. Now it's just a case of being patient and choosing a good supper.'

Now it so happened, that exactly the same thoughts were going through the shepherd's mind.

'I need a good supper tonight,' thought the shepherd, poking his fire and sharpening his knife. 'One of these sheep will do very well.'

Dusk was already beginning to blur the outlines of the flock and the shepherd knew he must make his choice quickly before darkness fell. Moving among them he spotted a sheep which looked particularly rounded and meaty. Quickly, he killed it and was about to drag the carcass to his fire when he saw what he had killed – a wolf in sheep's clothing!

Information for the teacher

1   There are various useful calendar references for this story. The 13th of the month is St Servatius's Day. This saint features in an old proverb to do with sheep shearing: 'Who shears his sheep before St Servatius's Day loves more his wool than his sheep.' (Servatius died in 384.)

    Alternatively, the story could be linked with an anniversary of a renowned storyteller, of which there are several in May: Baron Münchhausen was born on the 11th in 1720; Charles Perrault (author of 'Mother Goose') died on the 16th in 1703; Paul Dukas (composer of 'The Sorcerer's Apprentice') died on the 17th in 1935; Arthur Conan Doyle (of the 'Sherlock Holmes' stories) was born on the 22nd in 1859.

2 A most useful story to link with this one is that of the wolf of Gubbio. This creature had done a great deal of damage and killing and was being hunted by the people of Gubbio. One day St Francis was walking when he encountered this sly and ruthless wolf. He immediately treated it with respect, called it 'Brother Wolf', protected it and set about teaching a creature who knew no better how to behave to others.

Hymn suggestion

Come and Praise Vol 2 'All the animals' No 80

Prayer

Let us pray this morning that we may be given the strength to avoid sly and deceitful behaviour. Let us always be truthful, honest and straightforward. Let us remember that even if no one else knows we have done something dishonest, we do.

National Curriculum Cross Curricular Reference

English is well served by the dramatic possibilities of the story. In written work, pupils could experiment with stories with the same kind of moral.

Science could be involved in closer looks at the diets, needs, lifestyles, longevity, hardiness, etc, of both sheep and wolves. Geography could then be involved in locating places where ideal conditions for sheep rearing exist in the world.

There is also some scope for Music. Pupils could listen to 'Peter and the Wolf' and then work out some improvised music to act as background to a dramatised version of the story.

20 Thank you, doctor

Introduction

There are many reasons why we are lucky to be alive today rather than hundreds of years ago. One of them is that many people in the world now have excellent doctors, nurses, hospitals and medical care to see that they stay healthy and are treated quickly if they become ill. It was not always the case . . .

Story

It was a beautiful day in May 1347. The sun shone down on the sparkling waters of the Mediterranean Sea and the people of the Sicilian port of Messina went happily about their business. It was then that the eleven ships were seen at the harbour mouth.

'Look, those galleys must be from Genoa.'

'Yes, no doubt about that.'

'But . . . why aren't they steering properly?'

'They're all over the place.'

'They're crashing into each other!'

'They're not going to stop in time by the harbour wall . . .'

'No, they're ramming it!'

As if jerked about by unseen puppet strings, the eleven ships careered into each other, steered wildly erratic courses, and finally crashed brutally into the harbour wall.

The citizens of Messina put out in small boats to help, and boarded the galleys. There they found the reason for the strange behaviour of the ships.

Practically every member of the crew in each ship was dead, and those sailors still alive were desperately ill and not able to do their job properly.

'What is it?' 'What disease have you got?' 'How can we help?' These were the questions the survivors were asked.

But soon the people of Messina were no longer asking questions – they were too ill. A sudden and painful illness of three days was followed by death on the fourth day. Soon the mysterious illness was sweeping through Italy to Germany, France, England and the whole of the rest of Europe.

Towns and villages were wiped out and millions of people died. There were no well-trained doctors and proper medicines such as we have today and people believed all sorts of strange things would save them. Some kept goats in the house with them all the time, believing that the smell would keep out illness. Others believed spiders sucked away all poisons from their house.

Eventually the mystery illness passed, but not before it had killed forty-two million people in Europe.

Information for the teacher

1 The Black Death swept through Europe in the middle of the fourteenth century. It struck Britain in 1348. Agricultural labourers died in their thousands, crops withered, robbers roamed everywhere and 'normal' living was a thing of the past.

   It is thought that this bubonic plague started in China and was spread through Europe by ships which carried aboard locusts, fleas, rats and other vermin.

2 All religions concern themselves with the wellbeing of others and the healing of the sick. Biblical references related to such a theme could include Luke 17, 11–19 and Mark 7, 31–5.

3 Two saints could be examined in more detail in connection with this story: Saints Cosmas and Damian. Christians of Arabic birth, these third-century twins devoted their lives to medicine and to surgery, such as it was in their day. They were killed for their Christian beliefs, but remain the patron saints of medicine. St Luke too was a doctor, but is remembered more for his gospel writing.

4 For notes and leaflets on the National Health Service, the appropriate address is: Department of Health, Richmond House, 79 Whitehall, London SW1. Inquiries should be directed to the Information Division.

5 Useful May 'medical' anniversaries to link with this story are: the birth of Florence Nightingale on the 12th in 1820; the inauguration of Australia's Flying Doctor Service on the 15th in 1928; the birth of Edward Jenner, discoverer of vaccination against smallpox, on the 17th in 1749.

Hymn suggestion

Come and Praise Vol 1 'From the darkness came light' No 29

Prayer

Dear God,
Let us be thankful for good health, and let us pray for all those who don't have it. May they have the strength and will to recover.

   Let us also give thanks for the skills and knowledge of doctors and nurses, and those who find medicines to cure illnesses. Amen.

National Curriculum Cross Curricular Reference

There is plenty of scope for Science here – good practices for health, our bodies, etc. Both Geography and History could be involved in further study of the Black Death. The superstitions associated with it could provoke discussion in English.

21   The sisters

Introduction

This morning's story is one of unselfishness. It is about two sisters and their mother.

Story

Lily and Janet were twin sisters. They lived with their mother, many years ago. Their father was dead and the family did not have much money.

When they went to school both girls had a chance to sing – and they were a sensation.

'Have you heard Lily sing? She's wonderful!'

'She is, but I think Janet is even better.'

'No, you can't separate the two, they are both marvellous.'

So it went on. The girls sang together, and by themselves, and their fame spread from their school thoughout the village, and even to the nearby town. They sang in concerts and their mother was very proud of them.

One day they sang at a concert in another village. By now they were in their teens and quite used to performing. That evening, unknown to them, a famous singing teacher from Vienna was in the audience. After the concert he came to see them.

'That was delightful, girls. May I introduce myself? My name is Hans Gonert and I train opera singers. I think you could both become famous singers, but you need training. I'd like to take you both to my school in Vienna and teach you. I know you'll want to talk about this so I'll come and see you in the morning to discuss details.'

Lily and Janet could hardly contain their excitement. But as they walked home each had thoughts which were exactly alike, but which they didn't mention to the other.

Where was the money going to come from, to live in Vienna? Who was going to look after their mother, who was now getting old and frail, while they were away? Finally Lily spoke.

'It's a marvellous opportunity, Janet, but I think you're better than me and I'm not sure I want to go anyway. You go and I'll stay home.'

'Nonsense. You go and I'll stay,' replied Janet.

Being twins, and knowing what the other was thinking, the two girls suddenly stopped and threw their arms round each other. Both wanted desperately to go, but . . .

'I know the answer,' said Lily. 'We'll both go, but this is how we'll do it. First of all you go. I'll get a job here to help you out with the money and I'll stay and look after Mum. Then, when you've trained, you come back and I'll go and train.'

When the girls put this to Herr Gonert the next day, he accepted, and Janet went off to Vienna.

Meanwhile, back at home, the job which raised the most money to help pay for Janet's training was working on a market stall. Every day, in all weathers, Lily stood outside shouting her wares and working from almost dawn till dusk. Then she went home and looked after her mother. Each week she sent money off to Janet and each week she received a long letter back telling her about how wonderful the training was and what marvellous progress Janet was making.

Finally, after several years, Janet's training was over. The next day she caught the train for the long journey home so that Lily could take her place. Lily met her at the station and the two girls hugged each other silently for a minute.

'You'll love it, Lily,' said Janet. 'There'll be some great jobs when you've trained and Vienna is a lovely city.'

'I'm sure it is,' said Lily.

Janet looked at her sharply.

'Your voice, Lily! What's the matter with your voice?'

'Oh, it's nothing,' croaked Lily in her rough voice, 'but, you see, shouting in a market all day . . . well . . .'

'You mean, you can't . . . you can't . . .'

'No, Janet. It's gone, I'm afraid. I'll never be able to sing like you now, no matter how much I train.'

Janet looked at the tired but smiling face of her sister and felt the tears run down her face.

'Oh Lily . . . Lily.'

So it was. Janet went back to Vienna and became a famous opera singer and Lily stayed at home, worked in the market and looked after her mother. When Janet gave concerts she always dedicated one song on the programme to her sister Lily, and whenever Lily heard and read of her sister's fame she felt so proud.

Information for the teacher

1   The perfect location for this story is 20th May. This was the date on which the painter Albrecht Dürer was born in 1471. The story of Janet and Lily is loosely based on that of Albrecht and his brother, Franz.

    Albrecht and Franz were both painters. Franz, the elder brother, took a heavy labouring job to pay for Albrecht's studies on the understanding that the roles would be reversed when the Albrecht's studies were finished. Sadly, when this was the case Franz's hands were ruined by his work and he could no longer paint. As a testimony to his brother's sacrifice Albrecht painted a picture of his brother's hands clasped together in prayer. This magnificent and beautiful picture has remained world-famous ever since. It appears on many cards and would be a most useful acquisition as a teacher's resource.

2   Lily's hoarsened voice and Franz's ruined hands were, in a sense, beautiful because of what they acheived. Some quotations about beauty may be apt here:

    'Beauty is a combination of qualities . . .' (dictionary reference).

    'Beauty is truth, truth beauty' (John Keats, 1795–1821).

    'Judge not according to appearance' (St John, 7, 24).

Hymn suggestion

Come and Praise Vol 1 'For all the beauty of the earth' No 11

Prayer

Dear God,

Let us give thanks for those people who make sacrifices so that others can benefit. Let us give thanks for our parents and friends who want only the best for us and who try to help us and guide us.

    Teach us to value unselfishness and give us the strength to practise it. Amen.

National Curriculum Cross Curricular Reference

Music and Art are both obvious links with this story. Discussion on unselfish acts is also fruitful ground with groups of children, for English.

22　*Lightning strike*

Introduction

Before we go on to this morning's story, just pause for a moment and look at your closest friends who are near to you. Think about the fun you have together. Now listen . . .

Story

'That's some storm building up,' called Ben, pointing to the black clouds towering overhead.

'You're telling us,' replied Kieran. 'I reckon we're in for a real downpour.'

'Let's get a move on, then,' shouted the others.

There were six of them. All were aged fifteen or sixteen and they were on a self-reliance exercise, walking on the Brecon Beacons. They were part of a bigger group of over one hundred boys who had eleven teachers with them – but just at the moment this little group of six boys were walking by themselves.

Overheard, the black clouds moved slowly and threateningly. Deep growls of thunder boomed overhead and the darkness was lit by flashes of sudden lightning.

'I think we're going to miss . . .' Ben didn't finish the sentence. A sudden flash of lightning streaked earthwards and struck the metal necklace he was wearing. Without a word, he crashed to the ground unconscious.

'He's hurt!' cried Kieran Bowers, the leader of the party. Bending quickly beside his friend, Kieran noticed that not only was Ben unconscious, but he had stopped breathing as well. As fast as he could, Kieran placed his mouth over Ben's and began to give him mouth-to-mouth resuscitation. The other boys, seeing there was nothing they could do, raced away to give the alarm.

Kieran continued to work on his friend. As he did so, he noticed the severe burn around Ben's neck where his necklace was. Weakening from his efforts, at last he felt movement from the unconscious boy. He was breathing again, and it looked as if he was going to be all right!

It seemed that hardly had Kieran reached this stage than he heard a helicopter thundering overhead. Within seconds he was watching as Ben was carried aboard on a stretcher and whisked away to the Prince Charles Hospital in Merthyr Tydfil.

The story had a very happy ending. Ben was burnt round his neck and round his feet where the lightning went into the ground. He was suffering from shock. However, he was soon on the way to recovery.

One of the RAF helicopter experts said that if Kieran hadn't given immediate help, and if the others hadn't got the helicopter so quickly, Ben could well have died.

The story appeared in all the newspapers and both Kieran's mother and his headteacher said how proud they were of him.

Information for the teacher

1 This incident took place in May 1992 when the boys were participating in a self-reliance exercise at a specially prepared Ministry of Defence Camp. They had been well prepared in survival and emergency techniques, training which obviously had very beneficial results.

2 As a postscript to this assembly, a demonstration of mouth-to-mouth resuscitation could be given to the assembled children.

3 The value of reliable friends is very strongly emphasised by this story. A useful little tale to tell in contrast is that of the two boys who were walking along a forest path when they met a bear. One immediately bolted and left the other. The latter fell to the floor and lay motionless. The boy who had run away watched the bear bend over his friend's body, sniff it, apparently 'speak' and then lumber away.

When he got back to help, he said to his friend: 'That bear looked as if it was speaking to you.'

'It was,' replied the other, ' "Some friend you've got," it said.'

4 A useful address in relation to this story is: the Outward Bound Trust, Chestnut Field, Regent Place, Rugby CV21 2PJ. Taking things a little further, mouth-to-mouth resuscitation is often associated with accidents in water, and a useful book to have might therefore be: *The Blue Code for Water Safety*, issued by the Royal Life Saving Solciety, Mountbatten House, Studley, Warks B80 7NN.

Hymn suggestion

Come and Praise Vol 2 'I was lying in the roadeway' No 88

Prayer

Let us think this morning about the responsibilities of being a good friend. Are we reliable, honest, truthful, helpful, always on time and prepared to do what we say we will?

Let us pray that if we are ever called upon to prove our friendship we will be equal to it.

National Curriculum Cross Curricular Reference

There is a great deal of work here which can be linked to Science: health, the human body, weather, etc. This can be extended into Technology by examining what makes helicopters so useful in these situations.

Locating where the action took place is a useful geographical exercise. The story is one which lends itself to very 'dramatic' drama.

23   Fair shares

Introduction

As you know, most old stories have good and bad characters in them. It is possible, though, to have a story which is interesting even though there are only good characters in it. Perhaps you will agree after listening to this morning's story.

Story

Omar and Anwar were very sad. They were the sons of a farmer who had just died. Although their father had been old and tired, they missed him very much.

'He always gave us such good advice,' said Omar.

'Yes,' agreed his brother. 'Nothing was ever too much trouble for him. He was the kindest of men.'

So the two brothers opened the letter their father had left them.

> My dear sons [it said] thank you for all the happy times you helped me to enjoy over the years. I wish you both every happiness. If you go to the barn you will see that what I have left is divided equally between you.

So the two sons went to their father's big barn. He had asked one of his servants to stack his precious bags of corn against the walls. There was exactly the same number of bags in each pile. In front of one of them there was a little notice saying 'Omar'. In front of the other a notice said 'Anwar'.

'Just like him,' said Omar, 'fair and thoughtful to the last.'

'Yes, you're right,' replied Anwar.

Now, although both had been very good sons, they lived very different lives. Omar wasn't married and only had himself to think about. On the other hand, Anwar had a wife and three children.

That night, after they had got into their separate beds, the brothers lay thinking.

'I wonder if my father has been quite fair?' thought Omar to himself. 'He's left the same number of sacks to both of us – but I have only myself to worry about and I have all I need. Now, Anwar, he needs all he can get to care for those children of his. I think I'll go and rearrange our inheritance.'

So, slipping out into the bright moonlit night, Omar made his way to the barn. Leaving the door open to let the moonlight in, he dragged ten sacks from his pile and put them on Anwar's pile.

'Now, I feel better about that,' he said to himself. Then he went back to his bed and fell into a sound sleep.

Meanwhile, Anwar was tossing and turning in his bed.

'What's the matter?' asked his wife.

'It's my father's arangements for Omar and me. They just don't seem right.'

'What do you mean?' asked his wife.

'Well, I'm such a lucky man,' went on Anwar. 'I've got you and we've got our three lovely children. What more could we possibly want? Omar, he's just got himself. I think he deserves a bigger share than me.'

'I agree,' said Anwar's wife. 'But what can you do about it?'

'I'm going to creep over to the barn now and move some sacks from my pile to his. Nobody will ever know about it.'

So, as the moon continued to shine down, Anwar crept stealthily to the barn. Working quickly and quietly, he transferred ten sacks from his pile to Omar's.

Next morning, both brothers were up bright and early – for each had separately decided to go to the barn to check that they hadn't left any trace of their night-time visit.

When they reached the barn they met each other and were astonished to see that each pile had exactly the same number of sacks in it as on the day before.

(Adapted from a story in *The Caravan of Dreams* by Idris Shah.)

Information for the teacher

1   This story is ideal for this morning's calendar link, which is with the week of storytelling that the Federation of Children's Book Groups annually promotes in May. This event should be watched out for, particularly as one of the expressed aims of a recent such week was 'to reflect harmony among peoples and a wealth of cultural heritages.'

A contact address in connection with the Federation of Children's Book Groups is: Sue Bates, Old School House, Winterborne Houghton, near Blandford, Dorset DT11 OPD.

Hymn suggestion

Come and Praise Vol 1 'I listen and I listen' No 60

Prayer

Let us think this morning about the many stories we hear in our lives. Let us learn from the wisdom which is so often contained in these stories. Amen.

National Curriculum Cross Curricular Reference

English is an obvious point of contact here, with both oral and written storytelling a natural follow-on from material like this. A marvellous musical link could be the evocative *Sheherazade* by Rimsky-Korsakov, in which the music portrays the princess's endless storytelling.

24   *Mayday!*

Introduction

If we speak English we all know what 'Help!' means. Sometimes, however, it is important that a call for help can be understood in every language in the world. Listen carefully to this morning's story.

Story

'We're in trouble, Jack!' The pilot of the small two-seater plane flying over the dense jungle of Thailand called urgently to his friend in the passenger seat.

'What is it, Wilbur? What's the matter?'

'Port engine's gone – Look! – I can't hold her much longer.'

Looking out of the cabin window, Jack saw the propeller of the port engine whirling uselessly to a stop as he felt the plane keel over to an unnatural angle.

'We'd better call for help quick!' called Jack, changing the frequency on the radio.

'Mayday, Mayday, Mayday,' called Jack, as Wilbur struggled with the controls.

For hundreds of miles around, these three words alerted radio operators everywhere. Immediately, all other transmitters using the frequency closed down so that Jack could be heard clearly.

'Mayday, Mayday, Mayday,' called Jack again. Then, speaking slowly and carefully, he went on to give the name of his plane and the latitude and longitude of its position so that all listeners would know exactly where he and Wilbur were.

Instantly, on other radio frequencies, calls began to pass urgently back and forth.

'Small plane in trouble over area in Thailand.'

'Pilot about to crash-land.'

'Alert rescue helicopters.'

'Organise ground rescue.'

'Alert nearest hospital.'

'Have an ambulance standing by.'

So the messages went on and by the time Wilbur brought the plane down in a successful crash-landing dozens of people were preparing to rescue and help the two men. Fortunately, neither was badly hurt and within hours they were being cared for in hospital.

This story might not have had such a happy ending, however, if it had not been for a man called F S Mockford and the word 'Mayday'.

In the 1920s, Mr Mockford was the man in charge of all wireless services at Croydon airport. One of his first jobs was to invent an international alphabet for giving the registration number of aeroplanes clearly over crackly airwaves. For instance, he gave the letter T the name Tango; S was Sierra; B was Bravo. Therefore an aeroplane registered as TSB24 could give as its call-sign: 'Tango Sierra Bravo 24'.

Mr Mockford then wanted to think of a word which aeroplanes, or ships, could send out over their radios to show that they were in danger or distress. This word would have to be understood all over the world by people who spoke all different languages.

'Well, as the navy's distress signal is SOS, tapped out by Morse Code, why don't you just get the pilots to shout "SOS" into their microphones?' asked one of Mockford's officers.

'I'll tell you why – just listen.'

So an aeroplane was sent out and the pilot was asked to choose his time to say 'SOS' into the microphone. When he did, it sounded so blurred that it could easily have been missed by most listeners.

'You see what I mean?' said Mr Mockford. 'We've got to have a word which comes across clearly, without any mistake, and which everybody will recognise instantly.'

'Have you got one in mind?'

'Yes,' replied the wireless expert. 'It's "Mayday".'

'What a strange word,' said his friend. 'Why did you choose that?'

'It's really a French word – "M'aidez", which means "Help me",' went on Mr Mockford. 'And when you say it over the radio it comes out clearly and unmistakeably.'

And so 'Mayday' became the international distress call. Since then it has been used thousands of times by ships and aeroplanes and, without doubt, it has saved many thousands of lives.

Information for the teacher

1   The calendar location for this story is obvious. 'SOS' was first recognised internationally as a distress signal in 1906. The invention of a wireless telephone to enable pilots to talk in flight came about in 1919.

2   All religions advocate the helping of people in difficulties and there are plenty of examples to be found in Christian, Islamic, Hindu and Buddhist stories. The Good Samaritan is perhaps the best known from Christian sources, but there are plenty of Old Testament tales on the theme of help being sought and given. Included here could be Joseph and his brothers (Genesis 42); the crossing of the Red Sea (Exodus 14); Gideon and the Midianites (Judges 6–7); and David and Goliath (I Samuel).

Hymn suggestion

Come and Praise Vol 1 'Travel on' No 42

Prayer

Let us pray this morning for travellers wherever they may be. May their journeys be safe and may they reach their destinations fit and well. Let us give thanks for all those who have helped to make travelling safer and for those skilled in rescue when accidents occur. Amen.

National Curriculum Cross Curricular Reference

A further investigation into disasters could be involved in this theme. This could embrace subjects such as English, Science, Technology, History and Geography. Two very useful books of reference are: *A Book of Great Disasters* by P Drackett (Purnell) and *Timespan – Disasters* by Tim Healey (Macdonald).

25 *Once too often*

Introduction

'You've tried that trick once too often!' You might have heard a parent say that to a child who has been naughty. Your Mum or Dad might even have said it to you! This morning's story shows exactly what this comment means.

Story

Jake was excited.

'Maria,' he said to his wife, 'we'll definitely be able to earn more money if we do this. Then we'll have enough to mend the roof.'

'What are you talking about?' asked his wife.

'Well,' Jake went on, 'I've heard that you can buy salt really cheaply at the seaside. I'll go and buy a load, bring it back and sell it for a good profit at the market.'

'But how will you get it here?'

'That's easy – that's what I've got old Oscar for.'

Now, Oscar was the family ass. He did all the fetching and carrying to and from market. To tell the truth, he was a lazy creature and would do anything he could to get out of work.

The next day Jake set off with Oscar to the seaside where the salt was cheap. When they got there Jake bought the salt and loaded it in sacks which he strapped on Oscar's back.

'This is terrible!' thought Oscar. 'These are heavy and I've got to walk all the way home with them. What a life!'

The two set off on the return journey. At one point they had to walk along a steep and slippery path which ran alongside a fast-flowing stream. The grumbling and weary Oscar wasn't watching where he put his feet and with a sudden clatter he fell into the stream.

Concerned, Jake pulled him out. 'What a rotten fall,' he said, stroking the ass's head. 'I hope you're all right.'

Oscar kept his eyes fixed on the ground – he had made a wonderful discovery. When he had been in the water a terrific amount of the salt in the sacks had dissolved, and his burden wasn't even half as heavy now!

Next day, Jake took Oscar back to the seaside again so that they could get another load of salt. Trying to make good his loss, he got an extra sack this time. Oscar responded in his usual awkward way – until they reached the slippery path again. Then, with a great show of panic, he pretended to slip again and fell into the stream.

The same thing happened as before. Jake pulled him out, dried him off and consoled him. Meanwhile, Oscar smirked to himself and walked on with hardly any burden at all.

Next day they were off back to the seaside again. Jake busied himself buying and filling sacks. Oscar stood quietly, sure that he knew how to get the best out of this situation now.

'Rightho Oscar, off we go then.'

Jake had finished loading the sacks onto the ass's back and they were moving off along the familiar path home.

'That's funny,' thought Oscar, 'these sacks are much lighter than they were before. Maybe he's feeling sorry for me and just got a lesser load. Anyway, by the time I fall in the stream again it'll seem as if I'm carrying nothing.'

The journey went on until they reached the slippery path again. Once more Oscar managed to slip and splattered down into the water. Once more, Jake dragged him out and consoled him. But there was a difference: Oscar's load now seemed to weigh about ten times more than before he had fallen into the water.

'This is . . . this is terrible,' muttered the ass to himself as he laboured homewards with the heaviest load he had ever had to carry.

That night Jake and Maria were talking again.

'Did you solve the problem?' asked Maria.

'Oh yes,' replied Jake. 'I bought a load of sponges today and after he had fallen deliberately into the water his load was much, much heavier. I think our Oscar has learned his lesson – he tried his trick once too often.'

(Adapted from an old fable)

Information for the teacher

1   There are two possibilities for a calendar link with this story. It could be used on the anniversary of the French writer Charles Perrault, who died on 18th May 1703. He was a father in old age and published his children's tales ('Mother Goose', 'Bluebeard', 'Tom Thumb', 'Cinderella', 'Red Riding Hood' and 'The Sleeping Beauty') under his son's name.

   Another possibility is to link this story of 'trickery' with the date on which Jonathan Wild was executed – 24th May 1725. Jonathan Wild was acknowledged as a masterly tutor of thieves, tricksters, pickpockets and the like.

2   Another fable with a rather similar theme is 'Cry Wolf' which could be used for comparison with this one.

3   Any book of Aesop's fables is a useful resource for assemblies. Aesop lived in Greece about three thousand years ago. He was a slave whose stories of animals reflected both the virtues and frailties of people. Such was his skill as a storyteller that he was given his freedom from slavery. A concise paperback collection of the fables, edited by Ann McGovern, is published by Scholastic.

Hymn suggestion

Come and Praise Vol 1 'God knows me' No 15

Prayer

Let us think this morning about how we often try to make our lives easier by tricks and excuses. Let us learn to be straightforward in our dealings with people so that we are not embarrassed when our tricks and excuses are discovered. Let us pray that we always have a clear, and not a guilty, conscience.

National Curriculum Cross Curricular Reference

English could be involved in research into great storytellers of the past. This might embrace ancient Greece, via Aesop, and provide an historical link. The location of such stories also incorporates Geography.

26   Julie's story

Introduction

May is a month when people like to get home from work to enjoy gardens, parks and being outside. This morning's story is about a young woman who had had a very tiring day at work and was looking forward to getting home.

Story

'People think being an air stewardess is an exciting job, but it certainly is a hard one,' thought British Airways stewardess Julie Bird as the headlights of her car cut through the darkness of the unlit motorway.

She was going home at last after a very long day's flying when she had been on her feet for many hours at a time.

'I'll be glad to get home and get to bed,' she thought to herself.

Suddenly the car's lights picked up something on the motorway ahead. It was another car, standing in a lay-by, and there were two people beside it. Both of them were looking at the back of the car, which was sagging badly.

'I wonder if they need any help?' thought Julie at once.

She braked, and pulled her car into the lay-by.

'Hello,' said Julie. 'Have you got a problem?'

'Yes,' replied the man. 'A back tyre burst about ten minutes ago and I just managed to control the car and get into this lay-by. But I've just found that we've got no wheel brace – so we can't change the tyre.'

'We've been travelling for ages,' said the woman, who looked very, very tired. 'I don't know what we're going to do.'

Julie thought quietly for a moment.

'Well, my wheel brace won't fit your car, but I'll drive you to the nearest town and see if we can find a garage who can help.'

'Really – that's very kind of you – we hate to put you to so much trouble about this,' said the man.

It was now after ten o'clock in the evening and Julie was very tired herself. However, she didn't think of this as she pulled off the motorway with her two passengers and began to look for a garage.

She soon saw one, but it was closed. After half an hour's search she had found several more, but they were all closed too.

'Not much luck there,' she said as cheerfully as she could to her passengers. 'Why don't you ring the AA and see if they can help?'

So the man decided to ring the AA and Julie stopped at the first telephone box she came to.

'Thanks,' he said, getting back into the car. 'They'll come, but they might be quite a long time.'

'Don't worry,' replied Julie. 'I'll drive you back to your car and I'll wait there until the AA man arrives. Then if there are still any problems I'll be around to help.'

Once more Julie headed back to the motorway, and the couple's stranded car. There the three people waited until the AA patrol finally arrived – and changed the wheel.

'We don't know how to thank you for all your help,' said the woman to Julie. 'I just don't know what we would have done without you.'

'Oh, I'm just glad I could help,' replied Julie, giving them a wave as she drove off.

'Well,' she thought, 'on my way home at last.'

The story didn't end there. Some time later Julie was called into her manager's office and shown a letter. It was from the stranded motorists and they praised her 'kindness, generosity and courage'.

'Well done,' said the manager. 'You showed the qualities which helped us to choose you to be a British Airways stewardess in the first place.'

Information for the teacher

1 Stewardess Julie Bird was one of sixty British Airways cabin crew who received recognition at an Awards for Excellence presentation in Kites Restaurant, London, in the summer of 1992.

2 People disregarding hardship and danger for what they believe to be the benefit of others is a popular theme which permeates all religions. From a Christian point of view this story could lead on to some work on the journeys of St Paul. From his first missionary journey in AD 45 to his martyrdom in AD 65 Paul's actions and adventures provide great deal of useful material on this theme. A book and related work cards which could help are *Stories of the Early Church* (part of the *Introduction to the Bible* series) by R Horton and R Brandling (Hodder and Stoughton).

Hymn suggestion

Come and Praise Vol 2 'You've got to move' No 107

Prayer

Dear God,
We are just starting the morning of another new day. Please help us to make sure we use it well and do not let it slip uselessly away. Amen.
(Adapted from Thomas Carlyle)

National Curriculum Cross Curricular Reference

This story might provide an opportunity to study physical reactions when we are tired and when we are fresh. This could embrace Science and PE. 'Danger', 'courage', 'despair', 'saved', etc, are all words likely to stimulate discussion, lively writing and drama in an English context.

27   Down and out?

Introduction

There is an old saying: 'Beauty is in the eye of the beholder.' For instance, some people may see a chair as just something to sit on, others may think it is a beautiful piece of furniture. A teapot might be a precious ornament to one person – just something to make tea in to another. This morning's story makes us think about this.

Story

The German village was a very smart one. It was in the Alps and people came to ski there in the winter, and walk in the summer. The shops were fashionable and expensive – all except one.

Emma's shop was on the corner of two streets in one of the busiest parts of the village. It had been there for over a hundred years and Emma didn't like changes – everybody in the village called it *'Tante Emmas Laden'* – 'Aunt Emma's shop'.

'You never know,' said Emma to anybody who asked, 'something in this shop window might be just what somebody wants – or what somebody else thinks is really beautiful.'

Whomever Emma said this to always looked very doubtful when they saw what was in the shop window. It was piled high with old-fashioned record players, careworn musical instruments, ragged books, badly injured dolls, and so on.

For several weeks, high up in the right-hand corner of the shop window had been an old violin. The strings were tangled up and the wood was scarred. It didn't look as if it were worth much and it was impossible to think that it had once made music.

It was about this time that there came to the village a visitor quite unlike the smart crowd who were usually there. It was winter and, among the brightly coloured anoraks and the fur coats, the threadbare overcoat and thin shoes of this visitor looked very out of place.

He stayed in the cheapest place he could find and seemed only to walk slowly through the streets for daily exercise. Usually he stared at the ground but, on this particular day when passing *Tante Emmas Laden*, he happened to glance in the window.

It was as if he had seen something magical there. His head came up, a new and almost youthful look came into his eyes and he began to clasp and unclasp his hands eagerly. He went into the shop.

'Good morning,' said Emma.

'Good morning,' replied the visitor, 'I . . . I . . . could I have a look at the violin?'

Smiling, Emma reached over the piles of junk and got down the violin.

'Might have been quite good once,' she said.

But the stranger wasn't listening. With his head bent over the old instrument he was running a forefinger round the edging of the wood. Then, with finger and thumb he began plucking and gently tugging one of the strings.

Emma watched quietly. Seeing how captivated the old man was with the violin she began to get on with other jobs and left him alone. For more than an hour he stood there caressing and adjusting the old instrument. Then he spoke.

'Excuse me, but you don't happen to have a bow, do you?'

'One here somewhere,' said Emma, going on another rummage through the shop and coming up with a dusty-looking violin bow.

Slowly and carefully the old man tucked the violin under his chin and began to play. At once notes of clear calm beauty began to fill the shop. Emma stopped what she was doing and sat down. The music was beautiful.

After a few minutes the man stopped playing.

'Who are you?' asked Emma.

'Nobody,' replied the man. 'But when I was young I worked in Mittenwald where some of the world's best violins are made. When I looked in the window I was sure that this was one I had made many years ago – and I was right.'

He gently stroked the wood of the violin.

'Would you like it?' asked Emma.

'Oh I couldn't afford it,' said the man. 'I've been ill for a long time and I have no money. The doctor told me to come here for a few days for my health.'

At this moment the doorbell rang as another person entered the shop. It was Otto Lehrer, quite famous in the village and leader of the town orchestra which played, winter and summer, for visitors.

'Emma!' said Otto. 'I just heard the most fantastic violin playing coming from this shop – fantastic . . . '

Emma didn't speak, but just nodded her head towards the old man.

'Oh . . . well . . . ' he began to mutter.

'So it was you, sir. Well, a talent like yours doesn't come our way very often and we're looking for a lead violinist for the orchestra. The money's not bad and there's a tiny flat with the job – are you interested?'

'Well . . . it's wonderful . . . but, you see, the violin doesn't belong to me.'

'It does now,' said Emma, ' and thank you for paying for it with that wonderful music.'

Information for the teacher

1   There are many folk and traditional stories similar to this where violins, trumpets and other musical instruments come to life in the hands of a 'mysterious stranger'. Mittenwald, near the German border with Austria, is traditionally a great centre of violin-making. Craftsmen here have to serve a long and demanding apprenticeship in the art.

2   A useful calendar link with this story is 3rd May. It was on this date in 1899 that Johann Strauss, the Viennese 'King of the Waltz', died. This provides an excellent opportunity to introduce and end the story with some sweeping waltzes in which violins are so heavily featured.

3   Beauty – 'any of those qualities of objects, sounds, emotional or intellectual concepts that gratify the aesthetic nature ' (Funk and Wagnall) – is certainly something which could be followed up either in the assembly or later.

4   Among the many quotations regarding beauty, one which seems particularly apt for this story is by Robert Bridges: 'Beauty, being the best of all we know, sums up the unsearchable and secret aims of nature'.

Hymn suggestion

Come and Praise Vol 1 'For the beauty of the earth' No 11

Prayer

Let us give thanks this morning for the sights and sounds which give us so much pleasure. Let us be grateful to artists and musicians who help us to enjoy these things.

National Curriculum Cross Curricular Reference

The construction of, and the sounds produced by, violins, and indeed other musical instruments, offer considerable scope for Science and Technology. For Music, children could seek and experiment with examples on record and tape. The beauty of the written and spoken word could involve English. History might involve the development of the violin, and some geographical research might establish why Mittenwald is such a centre of violin-making.

28 The cheat

Introduction

Every year in June the world's most famous horse race takes place at Epsom in England. This is the Derby. This morning's story is about this race, a horse that ran in it, and two men.

Story

A huge crowd was packed on Epsom Downs racecourse. A hot June sun shone down, people selling drinks and food shouted their wares and there was the sound of good-natured voices everywhere.

'Roll up for the greatest race in the world.'

'Which horse is going to win?'

'Running Rein – it's a certainty.'

'Not a chance! Orlando – that's the one for me.'

The date was 1844 and a tall man in a top hat stood watching the surge of the crowds around him. This was Sir George Bentinck and his job was to see that cheating, in any type or form, did not take place anywhere on the racecourse.

Another man in a top hat was looking around too. This was the owner of the horse Running Rein. Mr Goodman – that was his name – was very anxious for the race to start, and equally anxious for it to finish. If his horse won he would be fifty thousand pounds richer. This was an enormous sum of money in 1844.

The horses left the saddling enclosure and moved to the starting line. The crowd got more and more excited.

'They all look good.'

'What a race this is going to be!'

'Get ready . . .'

'They're off!'

Kicking clods of turf behind them as they ran, the horses leapt from the starting tape and pounded towards Tattenham Corner – the bend before they entered the straight run up to the finishing line. The brightly coloured silks of the jockeys flashed in the sunlight as each rider crouched low over his horse's neck, urging it to even greater speed. The roar of the crowd got louder and louder as two horses began to widen the gap between themselves and the other runners.

'Come on, Running Rein!'

'Come on, Orlando!'

Neck and neck, the two racing animals galloped flat out towards the winning post – and then, suddenly, with a last desperate burst of speed, Running Rein edged ahead, and the race was won.

Sir George Bentinck watched with interest the speed with which Mr Goodman got his horse away from the winner's stand and out of sight. He was even more interested, and suspicious, when he noticed the brown stains where Running Rein had been standing.

'There's only one thing *that* could be,' said Sir George to himself as he swept his fingers through the stained grass. 'That's dye. But why would anyone want to put dye on a horse?'

So Sir George began an investigation which was to last a year. During this time he found out that Mr Goodman had bought some brown dye from a hairdresser in Regent Street in London. He also found out that Mr Goodman had used this to dye a horse's legs brown. The horse was a four-year-old called Maccabeus who had won many races. Once his legs had been dyed brown he became known as 'Running Rein' and because the Derby is for three-year-olds only he had a big advantage over all the other runners.

'Now I've got all this information, I can show everybody what a cheat Mr Goodman is,' said Sir George to his friends.

So the case came to court and the courtroom was packed with jockeys, owners, trainers and members of the public. Even in places as far away as Australia and America people had heard what was happening and were taking an interest. Sure enough, Sir George proved that Mr Goodman was a cheat and a liar, and that his horse was a fake. The result of the race was changed, Running Rein was disqualified and Orlando was placed first.

The man who had tried to win the world's greatest horse race by cheating now stood in disgrace.

Information for the teacher

1   This story could be linked to the Wednesday in early June when the Derby takes place every year.
2   The phrase 'honesty is the best policy' might be discussed in connection with this story. This could be extended to consider 'conscience' – whereby if we have done something dishonest and nobody else knows about it, nevertheless we do.

Hymn suggestion

Come and Praise Vol 2 'Make us worthy, Lord' No 94

Prayer

Dear God,
Help us at all times to resist the temptation to cheat in any way. Help us to be honest and truthful at all times. Amen.

National Curriculum Cross Curricular Reference

There is an enormous amount of Maths which can be linked to horse racing – weights of jockeys, speeds over certain distances, betting odds on the horses, etc. Science could be involved in a close look at horses – size, characteristics, diet, etc. A look at the history of the Derby would not only reveal social changes but also unearth other famous incidents, for example when the suffrage campaigner Emily Davison threw herself in front of the horses in 1913 and was killed under the hooves of the King's horse. Her aim was to promote the Votes for Women campaign by the publicity she would gain by disrupting the race.

29   *A wise man*

Introduction

This morning's story is about a man who was clever, funny and popular. Because of this three other men tried to 'catch him out'. This is what happened.

Story

When Nasr-ud-Din took his pupils to the mosque he always rode backwards on his donkey.

'Why do you do that?' asked one of his pupils.

'To keep an eye on you as you are behind me,' replied Nasr-ud-Din, 'and to make sure I am still leading you.'

Now, as it happened, three other men who fancied themselves as very wise, but who were not Muslims, saw Nasr-ud-Din riding backwards like this.

'How can anybody think this man is wise?' said the first man,

' "Stupid" would be my description of him,' said the second.

'Why don't we show him up for what he is?' went on the third.

So the three men went to the Sultan of Turkey and said that they wished to test the wisdom of this so called wise man, Nasr-ud-Din.

Now the sultan knew what a wit and joker Nasr-ud-Din was so he didn't quite know what to expect when he summoned his old friend to the palace. There the sultan ordered the three men to ask their questions.

'Tell me, sir,' said the first man, 'exactly where is the centre of the earth?'

Nasr-ud-Din smiled. 'That's an easy question to answer, my friend. The centre of the earth is exactly under the spot where my donkey has his right foot at the moment.'

The questioner gasped. 'But how can you know that?' he queried.

'It's quite simple,' replied Nasr-ud-Din. 'But of course if you want to prove it, get a tape measure and measure the earth. If you think my calculations are wrong, please come and see me again.'

The first man sat down in confusion, and the second stood up.

'My question is – how many stars are there in the sky?'

'Easy, my friend,' replied Nasr-ud-Din immediately. 'The same number as the hairs on my donkey.'

The questioner was taken aback by the speed of Nasr-ud-Din's answer. 'But you can't prove that.'

'I don't need to, my friend, but perhaps you do. Would you like to count both and see if I'm right?'

So the second man sat down, confused and embarrassed by all the smiling faces at the court.

The third man had watched all these goings-on with interest. He was determined not to be caught out in the same way. He stood up and with a wide, but false, smile, he said, 'Sir, may I call you "Hodja"?'

'Certainly. Most people do,' replied Nasr-ud-Din.

'Now, it's true you don't know me, isn't it?'

'Never seen you before in my life,' answered Nasr-ud-Din.

'Well then, tell me how many hairs I've got in my beard.'

'Oh that,' replied Nasr-ud-Din instantly. 'You've got as many hairs in your beard as my donkey has in his tail.'

This time, the third man smiled more widely. 'I'm going to ask you to prove that,' he said.

'Well that won't be difficult,' went on Nasr-ud-Din. 'What we'll do is this – we'll pull out a hair from the donkey's tail, then we'll pull a hair out of your beard and we'll count them as we go along. We'd better start straight away though – you've got a very big beard.'

Suddenly the third man didn't seem so keen to have the point proved or disproved in this way!

After Nasr-ud-Din had gone the three men were so impressed with his quick-thinking that they told the sultan that from now on they would become Muslims.

(Adapted from an old Turkish story)

Information for the teacher

1   Nasr-ud-Din is a great folk hero of the Middle East and the Balkans. Known for his quick-thinking, ready answers and wit, it is possible that this legendary figure lived between the fourteenth and fifteenth centuries.

   Nasr-ud-Din was given the honorary title of *Hodja*, which means a scholar who is particularly knowledgeable about the Qur'an. The Hodja would act as a preacher in the mosque (Khatib), a prayer leader (Iman) or a magistrate (Cadi).

2   A most useful calendar anniversary to link with this story is 8th June. It was on this date in 632 that the Prophet and founder of Islam, Muhammad, died. There are many Muslim stories concerning Muhammad. One of the most succinct tells of his dealings with people who were always complaining. When a man was bemoaning the fact that he had no shoes, Muhammad pointed out a man kneeling in the mosque – who had no feet.

4   It is useful and interesting to compare 'Hodja' tales with others where a 'message' is often transmitted with wit and style. Stories of Anansi, Brer Rabbit, and tales by Aesop and La Fontaine provide suitable material.

Hymn suggestion

Come and Praise Vol 1 'I listen and I listen'   No 60

Prayer

Dear God,
Help us to value good advice and the wisdom of others. Help us to be good listeners when something worthwhile is being said. Amen.

National Curriculum Cross Curricular Reference

Both History and Geography could be involved in taking a closer look at Turkey – its location, past, country, climate, towns, traditions. Music might be brought into this feature and Art too. The art of storytelling could be developed both orally and by written work in English.

30   *Getting over a bad start*

Introduction

Many people do very worthwhile things in life after making a bad start. This morning's story is about a man called Columba and he certainly knew about trouble!

Story

The fight which had taken place had left several men bruised and battered. There were more than a few black eyes and bleeding noses.

The king was furious. Surrounded by his courtiers he glared angrily at the man who stood in front of him. 'This is all your fault – and you know it. Look at the trouble you have caused!'

'Yes, Your Majesty,' said the man bowing his head. His name was Columba.

'When you borrowed that beautiful manuscript of the Bible you promised you only wanted to look at it,' the king went on.

'Yes, Your Majesty.'

'But that wasn't enough, was it? Oh no – you had to try and make a secret copy of it and when the owner found out he was very angry – and rightly so.'

'Yes, Your Majesty.'

'And as if that weren't enough, when he complained, you and your families started this . . . this quarrel . . . this fight!'

'Yes, Your Majesty.'

'Well, I've had enough of you, Columba. This is the last straw. Get your things packed and leave Ireland within the next two days. You are expelled!'

So Columba was expelled from his native Ireland.

With a group of his followers he got a boat and set sail for Scotland, landing on the island of Iona in the year 563.

'I've made enough mistakes in my life,' said Columba to his friends. 'I've got the chance of a new start here and I'm going to make sure I take it.'

So, as the months passed, Columba and the rest of the group built first of all a monastery, and then a cathedral. As they prayed in these, Columba realised that it was not enough to help people on the island; he must go across to Scotland and northern England and tell people there about Christianity.

So he sailed backwards and forwards to the mainland, helping people to be good neighbours, to care about each other, to be unselfish. and to remember that, even if they had made a bad start in life, it was never too late to change and do good.

Information for the teacher

1 Columba died in 597 and his feast day is 9th June. He is credited with spreading Christianity over the northern part of England as well as Scotland. The island of Iona eventually became a famous place of pilgrimage.

2 A further interesting piece of 'hearsay' concerning Columba is that a stone was supposed to mark his birthplace in Garton, Donegal. When Irish emigrants were about to leave the country, tradition had it that they went and slept a night on this stone, thus curing themselves of any incipient homesickness.

3 The idea of Columba's determination and persistence to get over the difficulties of being expelled from his native land could be conveyed in the following quotation from the Bible: 'Bless the Lord, my immovable rock – he gives me strength and skill'. (Psalm 144, 1)

Hymn suggestion

Come and Praise Vol 1 'The journey of life' No 45

Prayer

Dear God,
We all make mistakes but please give us the wisdom to learn from them. Teach us that it is never too late to make new starts. Help us to have the determination to do what we know is right, and resist the temptation of laziness. Amen.

National Curriculum Cross Curricular Reference

The locating of Iona, and its relation to Ireland, Scotland and England, would be a useful geographical exercise. Some research into the growth of the community on Iona would involve History. The theme of 'homesickness' is one which could provoke considerable discussion in English.

31   Peace is best

Introduction

This morning's story is about something which took place in a war long ago. The war was between the Greeks and the Persians and what you are going to hear took place four hundred and eighty years before Jesus was born.

Story

'We could defend this pass for ten years,' said the first soldier.
    'I agree,' said the other.
    'We've got all the food we need in the village behind us and this is the only way into Greece.'
    Hearing his soldiers talk like this, Leonidas, commander of the Greek army, was very pleased. The huge Persian army, which had swept all before it, was advancing fast, but Leonidas knew that here, at the mountain pass of Thermopylae, he could stop the advance.
    The pass was so narrow that only a few soldiers at a time could charge into it. The steep sides meant that the enemies' arrows

wouldn't be much good and Leonidas knew that the Spartan soldiers he had at the front of the pass were the best in the world.

'We'll hold out here until the Persians get tired and go home,' he said to his men.

Soon the mighty Persian army arrived. It numbered over a million men and as well as foot soldiers there were bowmen, horsemen and chariots. Xerxes, the Persian commander spoke to his men.

'Once we are through this pass we will be on our way to Athens, Corinth and Sparta,' he said. 'The world will be ours. Now, they've got only a few thousand men holding this pass, so let's get on with it.'

The great battle started, but the Persians got nowhere. Every time they attacked the narrow opening of the pass they were driven back. They couldn't go round it and the sides were so steep they couldn't get more men in. Xerxes got more frustrated and angry as each day went on.

After one particularly bad day, he sat in his tent eating his evening meal. Suddenly there was a commotion outside.

'What is it?' the commander called out.

Two soldiers entered. 'We've got a Greek outside, sir. He says he must see you – and it will be worth your while.'

For a moment Xerxes was tempted to have the Greek taken away as a prisoner but then he thought, 'What have I got to lose by seeing him?'

'Bring him in,' he said to the guard.

Twisting out of the guard's rough grip, the Greek came into the tent. He had a furtive, greedy look in his eye and Xerxes took an instant dislike to him. 'Well?'

The Greek didn't waste time. 'I know how you can win this battle.'

'Indeed? And how is that?'

'There's a secret path through the mountains which comes out at the other end of the pass. Leonidas has his poorest troops stationed there. For a small consideration I can lead a party of your troops along this secret path. Then they can attack the Greeks from behind while you attack from the front.'

Xerxes looked with contempt at this traitor – but he thought about how this would be the solution to his problem.

'Right,' he said, 'let's go into this in more detail.'

Two nights later, Ephialtes, the traitor, led some of the Persians' best soldiers through the stony, dangerous mountain path which led to the other end of the pass at Thermopylae. They reached the far end of the pass just as dawn was breaking. Just as Ephialtes had said, this was where the poorest soldiers in the Greek army were stationed. When they saw the approaching Persians they were so shocked that they ran away without putting up a fight.

Thanks to careful planning, the Persians now made a frontal attack on the pass. The confident Greeks were then horrified to find that there were Persians behind them as well. They could no longer hold out and in a short time the Persians had won the battle and were on their way to Athens.

Information for the teacher

1 Greece and Persia were at war in 490 BC but neither side could gain a conclusive victory. As a result both spent the next ten years preparing for the next clash. The Persian army's invasion began with the crossing of the strait known as the Hellespont (now called the Dardanelles). Two thousand six hundred ships were lashed together to form a bridge over which the great army crossed.

   The Persian victory at Thermopylae yielded them little. Within a year Pausanias, Leonidas's successor, defeated them at Thebes. Xerxes was killed and the Persians fled.

2 This kind of betrayal and treachery can be reflected in religious sources by the story of Judas Iscariot (Matthew 26, 14–16) and also that of Devadatta who was a cousin of the Buddha, jealous of his wisdom and therefore ever ready to harm him.

3 Another possible link for this story is the tale of the Greek siege of Troy, and their eventual victory through concealment in the Wooden Horse. A calendar link is provided by 21st June. On this date in 546 BC the Greek philosopher and advocate of peace, Thales, died.

Hymn suggestion

Come and Praise Vol 2 'Spirit of Peace' No 85

Prayer

Let us pray this morning for peace throughout the world. Let us pray that those responsible for the terrible things which happen in war are helped to see peaceful solutions to their problems. Amen.

National Curriculum Cross Curricular Reference

The stories of ancient Greece are a well-documented historical source and there are ample follow-up opportunities here. Locating of where the events of the story took place is a useful geographical exercise, and the story lends itself well to drama in several parts.

32   *The cooking pot*

Introduction

If you play a mean, nasty trick on somebody it often seems to come back eventually and hurt *you*. This morning's story shows this.

Story

'Oh dear, oh dear, oh dear,' thought Sunil to himself.

'No matter how hard I work I never seem to be able to get enough money to feed my family properly. Well, it's no good moaning. I'll just have to try and work harder.'

Now Sunil was a good man. He did work and what's more he helped as many people as he possibly could. Nothing was too much trouble for him. As a result, when the great goddess Durga heard his thoughts she decided to help him.

The next day he was working a long way from home. Late in the morning he sat down for a rest and dozed in the sun. The goddess Durga spoke to him.

'Sunil, take this pot – it will keep your family well fed for ever.'

'What . . . what . . .?' Startled, Sunil awoke suddenly – and found a cooking pot beside him.

'That was the goddess Durga speaking to me,' he thought, 'but what did she mean about the pot?'

He picked up the pot, looked at it, turned it round, and then tipped it upside down. At once rice poured from it. Every time he turned it upside down limitless rice poured out.

'This is fantastic,' muttered Sunil. 'My family will never go hungry again. Thank you, great goddess, thank you.'

After work, Sunil made his way home. It was tremendously hot still and he was tired and dirty. When he came to an inn with a water trough he thought he would go in for a wash before he got home.

'Can I wash as usual?' he asked the innkeeper.

'Yes, go ahead.'

'Oh – and while I'm washing, will you look after this pot, please? It is very, very precious.'

While Sunil was away getting washed the innkeeper looked at the pot.

'Hmm,' he muttered. 'He's never had anything precious in his life! What can be so special about this?'

Then he turned the pot upside down and found out!

'Fantastic,' thought the innkeeper. 'Fantastic – I could feed my family for life if I had this pot. Now, how to get it . . .?'

The innkeeper scurried off to the cellar and found a pot which looked exactly like the one Sunil had asked him to look after. He swapped the two over.

'Got my pot?' said Sunil when he'd finished washing.

'Right here,' answered the landlord.

Sunil hurried home with the great news. Imagine his feelings when he turned the pot over and out came . . . nothing!

'The only time this pot has left my side was when I stopped at that inn,' he thought. 'That innkeeper must have changed pots.'

Now, Durga the goddess had seen all this happen. She was furious – first of all with Sunil for his carelessness, and even more so with the mean and deceitful innkeeper. She spoke to Sunil. 'Another pot awaits you.'

Sure enough, there was another pot, just like the first. Joyfully, Sunil turned it over – and out leapt a group of evil spirits who gave him a beating. Desperately, Sunil righted the pot and they disappeared back into it.

'That was awful,' he gasped. 'But I'm sure Durga is guiding me to show me how I can get the first pot back.'

So saying, he set off for the inn again. Going innocently up to the innkeeper, he spoke as before.

'I'd like to wash, please. Would you look after my pot in the meantime? Please be careful with it – it's even more precious than the first one.'

The innkeeper could hardly wait until Sunil was out of the way. Greedily he turned the pot over – and out shot the evil spirits. Not content with giving him a good beating, they were about to tear his inn to pieces when Sunil, who had been hiding and watching, rushed back to get rid of them by turning the pot over.

'Thank you, thank you,' gasped the innkeeper. 'I'm sorry – you must know what I did to your first pot to do this to me. Please – let me give it back to you at once.'

The innkeeper hurried off and came back with the first pot. This time Sunil checked it – and sure enough, out came the rice again.

Because he was such a kind man, Sunil gave the innkeeper a large

supply of rice before he made his way home again. From that day
onwards he and his family never went hungry again.

Information for the teacher

1   Durga, the Hindu goddess, is the wife of the great god Shiva, and is
    also known as Sati, Kali, Ambika and Devi. She is the
    'all-comprehending one' whose hands hold 'delight and pain'. This
    story seems a very appropriate example of her twin characteristics
    of benevolence and fierceness.
2   Perhaps the calendar links for this story could be reflections of
    'unfairness' in the modern world, and the continuing need for
    peace, consideration for others and equal opportunities. June
    contains some tragic anniversaries of people who did not receive
    these things: on the 11th, in 1982, forty-two British soldiers were
    killed at Fitzroy during the Falklands War; on the 15th, in 1952,
    Anne Frank's diary was published – she had kept it from 1942 to
    1944, when she was sent to a concentration camp; on the 29th, in
    1925, a law was passed in South Africa banning all black people
    from holding skilled jobs.

Hymn suggestion

Come and Praise Vol 2 'I come like a beggar' No 90

Prayer

Let us think this morning about fairness for all. Let us never begrudge
or be envious of the good fortune of others and let us always be
prepared to share our own good fortune. Amen.

National Curriculum Cross Curricular Reference

There is some geographical scope for links with India in connection
with this story. It is an excellent one for drama – and could encourage
play writing. It might also provide an opportunity for listening to some
Indian music.

33   Sarah Gooder's story

Introduction

For most children living in England today it would be hard to imagine what life was like for someone the same age one hundred and fifty years ago. Sarah Gooder's story gives us some idea.

Story

The men in the room were all silent. Then one of them spoke.

'Well sir, that's how it is. We need somebody to help us. Will you do it?'

The man who spoke had a tired, careworn face and his clothes were poor and well worn. His friends, who gathered round him, looked very much the same, but all had a look of absolute determination on their thin faces.

'If what you say is true, I promise that I will find out all I can about the situation – and do my utmost to put it right.'

The second speaker looked very different from all the other men. He was tall and elegantly dressed and his voice was calm and educated – but he too looked worried by what he had heard.

The tall, well-dressed man was the Earl of Shaftesbury and on this day in 1832 he had met a group of working men to hear what conditions were like in mines and factories all over the country. What he had heard had made him almost ill with its dreadfulness.

'There's women and children working in coalmines for sixteen hours a day. They never see the light of day and they're treated like slaves. It's the same in factories, where some children are so tired after sixteen hours working at a machine that they just fall to the floor and sleep. How old are these children? you ask. Well, some of them are only four.'

This is what one of the men had told Lord Shaftesbury. As soon as the group had gone, he began to think of how he could deal with this problem. He realised that he would have to find out exactly what was happening, prove it, and then get Parliament to pass laws to protect these desperate children.

So began a life's work for Lord Shaftesbury. First of all he visited coalmines and investigated conditions for the workers there. It was while he was preapring his first report on Children's Employment Conditions that he met Sarah Gooder. This is what she told him.

'The worst thing about my job is that I'm scared of the dark and it's dark all the time. I'm so scared I daren't even sing to cheer myself up.'

Lord Shaftesbury asked, 'How long do you work each day, Sarah?'

Sarah replied, 'I'm not really sure. I know that I get to the coalmine at half past three in the morning of each day and I work there until half past five in the afternoon.'

'Have you got a hard job to do?' asked Lord Shaftesbury.

'I've got to open and close ventilators in the mine all day,' said Sarah. 'That's not such a bad job – some of the other children have worse jobs. Jenny and Violet have to drag trucks of coal. They've got to do this crawling on their hands and knees because the roof is too low for them to stand up. It's too low for ponies to drag the trucks, so they have to do it.'

Lord Shaftesbury asked Sarah what she did when she was not at work.

Sarah replied, 'I just sleep. I'm too tired to even eat. I fall asleep over my food. I'm always tired. I never ever play – and I've got nothing to play with, anyway.'

'How old are you, Sarah?' asked Lord Shaftesbury, and she told him, 'I'm eight.'

Lord Shaftesbury wrote his report about Sarah and the other children, and people were absolutely horrified when they read it. There was a great uproar and people demanded that the Government should do something to stop these terrible things. Eventually Parliament ruled that no women or girls should ever work in mines again, and boys had to be ten before they could do so.

Information for the teacher

1   Legislation to prevent children working in mines was difficult to achieve because many of those who sat in the House of Lords were wealthy mine owners. In Lord Shaftesbury's diary there are entries like this one: 'The object of years within my grasp . . . a notice to investigate the condition of all the wretched and helpless children in collieries . . . I must have public knowledge and public opinion working within it.'

2   Children may be aware of the famous statue of Eros at London's Piccadilly Circus. They are less likely to know that this stands over a memorial to Lord Shaftesbury, symbolising Christian charity.

3   There are several calendar links which can be made with this story. On 6th June 1844 the Factory Act of England established an Office of Factory Inspectors whose job was to ensure the health and wellbeing of those employed in factories. Charles Dickens died on 9th June 1870.

Dickens was poor in his youth, and in his many novels he highlighted the desperate plight of poor children. Another link could be with 15th June, which is World Children's Day.

4 All religions advocate care and concern for children. Perhaps the most famous Biblical reference to children is in St Mark, 10, 14: 'Suffer the little children to come unto me, and forbid them not: for of such is the Kingdom of Heaven.'

5 A useful address is: Public Relations Department, British Coal, Hobart House, Grosvenor Place, London SW1X 7AE.

Hymn suggestion

Come and Praise Vol 1 'From the darkness came light' No 29

Prayer

Let us give thanks this morning for people like Lord Shaftesbury who, by their hard work, determination and concern, have made the world a better place for others.

National Curriculum Cross Curricular Reference

Pupils could investigate the history of mining (material from British Coal is very helpful here). Geography could also be involved in locating mining areas. Science and Technology can obviously be involved, with the investigation of how mining is carried out, the machinery used, geology, etc.

This story is one which can provoke considerable discussion, including the continuing hardships of working in mines. It is suitable for drama. Music could be involved by listening to, and improvising, 'work songs': a suitable record could be 'Working in the coalmine' by Lee Dorsey.

34 Gehazi's story

Introduction

When you do somebody a good turn you don't expect something in return – or do you? Listen to this morning's story.

Story

Many years ago there lived a man called Elisha. He was a special person who told others how God wanted them to behave.

Elisha was famous and one of those who had heard of his work was the chief of the Syrian army. This chief was called Naaman. He was a great soldier and an honest and reliable man, but he suffered from a terrible disease called leprosy.

One day his wife told him that one of her maids had said to her that there was a man in Israel who could cure his leprosy. At once Naaman set off to see this man, who was of course Elisha. When Naaman arrived, Elisha sent one of his servants to him with a message.

'My master says that you must dip yourself seven times in the River Jordan,' said the servant. 'If you do this you will be cured of your leprosy.'

'What a strange cure,' thought Naaman. However, he did as he had been told and, to his astonishment and delight, he found himself cured of the disease. He couldn't wait to get to see Elisha to thank him.

'Sir,' said Naaman to Elisha when they met, 'I cannot thank you enough for your help. I would like to take some of the soil of Israel back with me to remind me of the God you worship, and I would like to give you these gifts as my personal thanks to you.'

As he said this Naaman pointed to where his servants held donkeys laden with gold, silver and fine clothes.

'No, no thank you,' replied Elisha with a smile. 'I try to do God's work, that is reward enough. Please take your gold, silver and fine clothes back with you. I am sure there are many people in need of help in your country.'

Naaman thanked Elisha again and marvelled at what a kind and honourable man he was. 'As you wish,' he said. 'But thank you again.'

And so he set off to return to Syria.

Now, while this conversation between Elisha and Naaman had been taking place, Gehazi, Elisha's servant, had been listening and watching very carefully.

'My master might not want all those magnificent things,' he thought, 'but if I could get my hands on them I'd be rich for life – no more money worries, ever.'

So, allowing Naaman to get an hour or two on his way, Gehazi then went after the Syrian chief at great speed. He soon caught up with the little procession.

'Sir, sir,' called out Gehazi.

'Why, it's Elisha's servant. What can I do for you?' asked Naaman.

'Is something wrong?'

'No, no, sir, nothing is wrong . . . but it's like this. Two men have just arrived at my master's house and he wants to give them gifts. Well, he has nothing to give them and then he thought of you . . . and . . . '

'Of course,' said Naaman. 'I quite understand. It will be my pleasure. Please, take what you will and once again give your master my good wishes.'

So by this lie Gehazi got some of the treasure for himself and when he returned home he hid it away carefully.

But Elisha had missed him and it was not long before he found out what had happened. He sent for Gehazi.

'That was a terrible thing to do,' he said, 'you did not need Naaman's gifts. Now you have lost all you had.' And he sent Gehazi away with nothing.

Information for the teacher

1   This is an adaptation of the story of Elisha, Naaman and Gehazi which can be found in II Kings 5, 15–27.

2   A useful calendar link for this story could be 15th June, which is World Children's Day. This might focus thoughts on the real 'treasure' of life – family, friends, health, etc, as opposed to material possessions. A useful quotation in this context is the often 'misquoted quote' which should read: '*The love of* money is the root of all evil.' (I Timothy 6, 10)

3   Leprosy can now be cured by treatment. The Hebrew word *zara'ath* was translated in the Bible as 'leprosy'. The description of the disease in Leviticus 13 implies however that several diseases were covered by the word *zara'ath*, and these included various fungus type infections, and possibly things like psoriasis.

Hymn suggestion

Come and Praise Vol 2 'I come like a beggar' No 90

Prayer

> Father, we thank you for the night
> And for the pleasant morning light,
> For rest and food and loving care,
> And all that makes the world so fair.
> Help us to do the things we should,

To be to others kind and good,
In all we do, in all we say
To grow more loving every day.
Amen.

National Curriculum Cross Curricular Reference

This story is very well suited to drama. The scientific link could be with
health, caring for our bodies, the uses and value of water etc.

35   The disappointment

Introduction

This morning's story is a true one about someone who is an old man
now. He has had a very happy life and done lots of interesting things –
but he has never forgotten what happened once when he was a
schoolboy, as you will hear.

Story

John loved cricket. Whenever he had the chance he watched adults
play and he practised as hard as he could every summer. The trouble
was, he was not a really good player and although he had good days he
was never given a chance in the school team . . . until one day.

Before every Thursday afternoon's match the list of boys in the team
was pinned up on the school noticeboard. Every Thursday morning
playtime, John went along and read the names in the team. Although
he went to every practice his name was never there.

On one lovely June morning John knew that there was a home
match for the team that afternoon.

'I'm sure I won't be playing – but I'll go and have a look anyway.'

The noticeboard was in a particularly dark part of the school and
people had to get close to read what was on it. When John reached it at
playtime he found the usual crowd jostling round. As one boy broke
away from it, he called out to John.

'See you're playing this afternoon.'

John thought this was some sort of nasty joke but when he had
edged into the crush so that he could see the board, there it was – in
the middle of the batting order – his name!

For the rest of the morning John could hardly concentrate on his work. His greatest dream had come true. It didn't matter that he had got his place because some of the regulars were on a school trip. He was in the team! What's more, he had a feeling that all that practice was going to pay off. Yes, he felt he was going to score some runs today.

Dinnertime passed in a haze. A couple of his friends said how pleased they were for him and he smiled his thanks. Most of the afternoon before the match was spent doing art. Every five minutes or so John looked out of the windows at the pitch. At about a quarter to two the caretaker came out, put the stumps in place and marked out the pitch.

It must have been about ten past two when the first raindrop hit the window. It was followed by another, larger one and soon the window streamed as the tears of rain ran down. As John peered anxiously out, the outline of the stumps blurred and the sky darkened by the minute.

It was near to half past when there was a knock on the door and a messenger came in.

'Please, Miss, Mr Clarke's sent me to say that this afternoon's cricket match is off.'

As John peered through the streaming windows he saw the raincoated caretaker re-appear and yank out the stumps. He could feel his disappointment almost like a pain. He was never chosen for the school team again.

Information for the teacher

1 This morning's story is a true one and although it happened to the subject almost fifty years ago it remains a very clear memory. Usually children receive this story very attentively and thoughtfully and it is a useful and relevant way of reminding them that all lives have disappointments in them. The next point – for discussion and reflection – is how one reacts to disappointments.

2 A useful follow-on to this story, or indeed an addition which might be made to the assembly, is for the children to relate at first-hand some disappointments they have suffered. In these days of such social upheaval some sensitive awareness and tact on the part of the teacher may be called upon here.

3 The assembly might be enhanced by some taped cricket radio commentary being played, or some videoed TV test match coverage. Some bats, stumps, balls, etc, could also be on display.

Hymn suggestion

Come and Praise Vol 2 'It's a new day' No 106

Prayer

Dear God,
Please help us to treat the ups and downs of our lives with cheerfulness and patience. Let us not fall into the trap of boasting about our successes and moaning about our disappointments.

Please help us to be the sort of people who can help and encourage others at all times. Amen.

National Curriculum Cross Curricular Reference

A more detailed study of cricket could incorporate History (when it was first played), Geography (where it is played), and Science and Technology (how it works). Physical Education is of course another obvious link. Cricket, and indeed other games, often stimulate intensely interesting stories from children. There are also examples which could be read to them, especially Michael Hardcastle's sports stories.

36   Keep on trying

Introduction

Sometimes, when things seem very difficult, we are tempted to say, 'I give up.' This morning's story is about some people who wouldn't give up.

Story

It was a bright June day and the air high up in the Lake District was fresh and inviting. It was perfect for walking and Charles and Muriel Leeming were enjoying the exercise as they strode out on the high ground.

'What a day!' said Charles.

'You're right – and what a view,' answered Muriel, pointing to the countryside six hundred feet below them.

Torver, their eight-year-old Yorkshire terrier, let out an excited bark. He was certainly enjoying himself too.

The two people and their dog continued on their way.

'That's Clough Head Peak up there,' said Charles.

'Yes, one of the best spots on Helvellyn,' replied Muriel.

'Look at Torver, he's going to beat us to it!'

'He would . . . but that path's very narrow. Torver, be careful, be caref—'

Charles's voice petered out as, up ahead, the little dog suddenly lost his footing on the narrow path. With a scattering of small stones and a desperate yelp, he scrambled to pull himself up – and then suddenly he was gone. Charles and Muriel leaned helplessly over and watched their pet roll side over side down the slope of jagged scree. Twice he bounced off clumps of bushes and then, under the flying dust and stones, he disappeared.

'Oh Charles,' murmured Muriel tearfully, 'the poor, poor little chap.'

For the rest of the day the Leemings searched for their pet. Unfortunately they heard nothing from him, nor could they find him anywhere.

'I'm afraid he must have died in the fall,' said Charles, 'and perhaps his body is trapped in a crevice somewhere.'

Miserably, the two walkers returned to their home in Lancashire. Next day they described the incident to their local vet, Mr David Higginson.

'How awful for you,' said Mr Higginson. 'But you know, these Yorkshire terriers are tough little fellows. He might have survived the fall, but, being dazed, just wandered off somewhere.'

'But what can we do?' asked Muriel. 'Where do we begin to look for him?'

'Well look, leave it to me,' Mr Higginson went on. 'I have an idea. It may come to nothing but it's worth a try.'

So Mr Higginson got in touch with a vet he knew in Keswick, which was near where the Leemings had been walking. When he explained what had happened, the Keswick vet said he knew of an animal charity nearby which might be able to help.

When they heard the story they moved into action straightaway. Posters were given out containing the details of Torver, and his story was told in local newspapers and broadcast on the radio. Hundreds of people were on the lookout for the missing terrier.

Then, five days later, all the effort and determination put into the search for the little dog paid off. Four miles from Keswick a man spotted a particularly battered and bedraggled Yorkshire terrier lying under a caravan. When he was encouraged to come out he walked with a limp but didn't seem badly hurt. Yes – it was Torver.

Information for the teacher

1 Torver was returned safe and sound to the Leemings. His story received considerable publicity, and a photograph was published of the dog looking fit and well and reunited with his owners.
2 This theme of determination, not giving up, and pressing on regardless of discouragement is one which could be followed up by compiling a selection of stories which reflect these qualities in varying ways. National and local newspapers are useful here and many folk tales reflect the same virtues.

> Biblical stories which might be used here could include Noah and the Flood (Genesis 6–8); Daniel in the Lion's Den (Daniel 6); Moses in the basket of reeds (Exodus 2); David and Goliath (I Samuel 17); and Paul's journeys (Acts 13–28).

3 A useful address is: Countryside Commission, John Dower House, Crescent Place, Cheltenham. For those near enough, the National Park Centre at Brockhole in the Lake District is open to school parties and would provide first-hand local 'colour' relating to the story.

Hymn suggestion

Come and Praise Vol 2 'Let the world rejoice together' No 148

Prayer

Dear God,
We ask this morning that you may help us to be determined and caring, able to cope with disappointments, and to be reliable people at all times.

We give thanks for the many lives that are saved because of these qualities. Amen.

National Curriculum Cross Curricular Reference

Geography could be involved in research into the Lake District – its size, features, terrain, climate, dangers, etc. Science could be involved in studying survival in the condition described in the story. The story could be acted out in several scenes and there are some interesting creative writing possibilities in rewriting it from the dog's point of view.

37 *Trees*

Introduction

June is a month when it is lighter than at any other time of the year in the British Isles. This means we can spend more time outside looking at things – trees, for instance.

Trees

A poet, who is not very well known, once wrote two lines which have become very well known. They are:

> Poems are made by fools like me,
> But only God can make a tree.
> (Joyce Kilmer)

June is a good month not only for looking at trees, but also for learning about some of the more famous ones in the British Isles. For instance, some of them act as sort of signposts in our history.

Yew trees are often found in churchyards. One of the reasons for this is that their foliage is poisonous to cattle, so they were planted to keep cows from straying among the graves. The oldest yew trees in England are supposed to surround the small church in Westbourne, Sussex. These were planted by the Earl of Arundel in 1544, which is almost half a century before the great battle with the Spanish Armada.

If you go to Richmond Park, near London, you can see some of the oldest oak trees in England. Five of them were already there when Charles I first made this a park in 1637. Another very famous oak tree is at Boscabel. It was in this tree, after the Battle of Worcester, that Charles II hid from the Parliamentarian army. When he eventually returned to be king, people celebrated by carrying round oak tree branches to remind themselves of how he was once saved.

One of the most dreadful things ever to happen in England was the Great Plague in 1665. This caused many people to die, but one group supported each other by meeting under a tree. This tree was a sycamore tree near Mapperton in Dorset and a plaque was put up there which said: 'In 1665 when the Great Plague reached its peak, the parishioners gathered under this tree holding posies of flowers and herbs to ward off the disease.'

Then there is the famous Holy Thorn tree at Glastonbury Abbey. This blooms every Christmas and there is an old story that the first tree grew when St Joseph visited the spot and stuck his staff into the ground.

Although only God can make a tree, we should remember that if we are to go on enjoying the beauty of our trees it is up to us to take care of them and protect them. Here is a short poem to remind us of this:

> Woodman, spare that tree!
> Touch not a single bough!
> In youth it sheltered me,
> And I'll protect it now.
> (G P Morris)

Information for the teacher

1   The information contained here could be used to 'flesh out' a fuller assembly in which conservation is the wider theme. This could bring in things like acid rain, the destruction of too many trees, and issues which many children are both familiar with and concerned about.

2   Another direction in which this assembly might go is to look at local trees if this is appropriate. There may be a local park in which trees have been planted as memorials to local or well-known people, for example. Useful work could stem from a situation like this.

3   Useful addresses are:

Council for Protection of Rural England, Warwick House, 25 Buckingham Palace Road, London SW1W OPP;

The Countryside Commission, John Dower House, Crescent Place, Cheltenham;

The Conservation Trust, 246 London Road, Earley, Reading R66 1AJ. (This organisation is a source of information on various matters, including, specifically, trees.)

4   Trees are significant factors in the Bible – beginning with the one of such influence in the Garden of Eden (Genesis 2, 9; 3, 22–4).

In the arid deserts of Palestine trees were at one time considered sacred and have always been treasured.

In Christian art and tradition various trees have differing

symbolic meanings: the almond symbolises the Virgin Mary; the leaves of the aspen are supposed to tremble continually because it was the only tree which failed to bow in sorrow when Jesus died on the cross.

The cedar symbolises Jesus; the elm represents the faith of good Christians; the oak is one of several trees looked upon as the source of Christ's cross; the palm symbolises victory, and is particularly associated with Jesus' entry into Jerusalem; the olive is associated with peace.

Hymn suggestion

Come and Praise Vol 1 'For the beauty of the earth' No 11

Prayer

Dear God,
Thank you for the trees which grow in our countryside, parks and gardens. Help us to admire their beauty and to make sure that we care for them as well as we can. Amen.

National Curriculum Cross Curricular Reference

Practically every subject can be linked to this theme. The material already provided could stimulate thought in History and Geography. Caring for trees on a wider scale could embrace Science, with a particular emphasis on Environmental Education. Technology and Physical Education could be involved in thought on 'using' and 'climbing' trees. Trees are a popular choice for poems and, as well as listening to some, the children might write some of their own on the subject. Art is particularly well served by some outdoor painting of trees.

With regard to Music, improvised work could be related to specific trees and pupils could make a collection of songs and/or tunes related to trees – 'Trees', ''Neath the shade of the old apple tree', 'Hearts of Oak', etc.

38   *A life to treasure*

Introduction

We all get a great deal of pleasure from people who entertain us. They might be footballers, musicians, actors, artists or magicians. This morning's story is about a man who wrote wonderful music – but whose life was strangely bound up with the sea.

Story

The Russian warship *Prokhor* was wallowing in very rough seas. These were the days when ships were driven by sails and the captain gazed anxiously upwards.

'There's only one way to get out of this trouble,' he called. 'Send someone aloft to get more sail unfurled.'

An officer sprang to obey his orders. 'You – you – and you,' he shouted to three seamen. 'Get aloft on the mainsail.'

Slowly the three men climbed high up into the masts of the ship. One was a young cadet named Nikolay. The wind howled and shrieked round them as if trying to tear the clothes from their bodies. From one side to the other the ship yawed wildly and all three struggled desperately to hold on as their hands grew numb with cold.

'Get along and unfurl that sail,' shouted the senior sailor to Nikolay.

Inch by inch the young cadet edged his way through the swaying rigging.

'Nearly there,' he thought to himself. Suddenly the ship lunged violently to one side. One second Nikolay was reaching to unwind the ropes binding a sail – the next he was plunging downwards through the storm-lashed darkness.

Before he had time to think, he crashed into the pounding waves and sank rapidly. The freezing water filled his mouth and ears as he fought to swim back to the surface. No sooner had he done so than tough hands hauled him back on board.

'You were lucky there, son,' said one old seaman. 'Most people who fall off the rigging like that hit the deck – and that's the end of them.'

After his miraculous escape, Nikolay continued his career at sea. A new interest was taking up more and more of his time, however. He had bought a harmonium and every spare minute he was off duty he composed music. Tune after tune flowed out from his small instrument and finally he realised that he wanted to spend the rest of his life making music.

'As soon as I get back to St Petersburg I'm going to give up the sea and see if I can compose more,' he thought to himself. And so he did. Within a year he had written a great symphony which was soon performed. Then followed a second symphony and an opera.

Success followed success. Nikolay got married and was appointed Director of a School of Music. It seemed as if he just couldn't stop writing great music – and then one morning he got up with a strange feeling.

'I can't think of anything,' he thought to himself. 'There are no musical thoughts coming into my head.'

The next days was the same – and the next – and the next.

'I'm finished,' thought Nikolay. 'I've got no ideas left. I might as well give up. I've got nothing left.'

So he gave up his home in the great city and went to live in Odessa, a town by the sea. There he began to take long, lonely walks by the sea on which he had once earned his living.

One day, as he was walking along the beach, the tide was ebbing out slowly. As he watched the swirling water and heard it hissing on the sand he suddenly felt a tune forming in his mind again. Rushing home, he set about composing it properly. It was as if the sound of the waves had set his mind off again and never again had he any difficulty in writing great pieces of music.

The rest of Nikolay's name was Rimsky-Korsakov and you will almost certainly have heard some of his music. Now is your chance to listen to some more, knowing a bit about the man who wrote it.

Information for the teacher

1 The last sentence of the story provides an opportunity (if appropriate) to listen to some of Rimsky-Korsakov's work. There is plenty to choose from and among selections which seem most appropriate for primary school children are 'The Flight of the Bumble Bee', *Sheherazade*, and *Sadko*.

2 The reason for linking Rimsky-Korsakov with this month is that he died on 21st June 1908.

3 There is a very telling quotation about music in Shakespeare's *Merchant of Venice*. It is obviously for adult consumption but a little tactful adaptation by the teacher could certainly get its message across to children:

    The man that hath not music in himself,
    Nor is moved with concord of sweet sounds,

Is fit for stratagems and spoils;
The motions of his spirit are dull as night,
And his affections dark as Erebus:
Let no such man be trusted.

Hymn suggestion

Come and Praise Vol 1 'A living song' No 72

Prayer

Let us give thanks this morning for those composers whose music has given so many people so much pleasure.

Let us give thanks, too, for musicians everywhere whose skill and talents help us to enjoy music. Amen.

National Curriculum Cross Curricular Reference

Music is the obvious link here with opportunities to listen to more of Rimsky-Korsakov's work and to improvise music to suit the various moods of the sea described in the story. Storytelling is an obvious link with *Sheherazade* and this could be developed along the theme of the princess telling stories which whet the appetite for more and more.

39 *An early hero*

Introduction

Imagine this morning that a radio reporter has entered a time/space capsule. He has been taken back to a town in England called Verulamium and the time is between two and three hundred years after Jesus was born.

Story

'Good morning, listeners. I've been sent here this morning on a Time/Space mission to find out more about an event which happened hundreds of years ago.

'I must admit I've been very impressed with this town. The Romans have really made a good job here – it's a busy place with some splendid buildings and there are plenty of theatres, temples, houses and shops.

'Ah – but this is what I have come to report on. As I speak, there's a huge crowd of people heading towards the river. There's a group of Roman soldiers in the lead and in front of them they are pushing a man who has obviously been badly treated. Behind are lots of people of the town. I'm going to try and have a few words with one of these . . .

'Excuse me, sir, can you tell me what's happening here?'

'Well, as much as I know, yes. That poor fellow who is getting pushed around up there is called Alban and he's being taken to the river to be executed.'

'That's terrible! But what has he done?'

'On the one hand, not much, on the other a great deal. You see, just a few days ago he was just an ordinary citizen of the town, like me. Now in this town there is a group of people who call themselves Christians. Naturally the Roman magistrate wants to get rid of these people because he thinks they are troublemakers.

'Well, last week one of these Christians was on the run from some soldiers and the only place he could find to hide was Alban's house.

Apparently the two men talked long into the night and by the time they had finished Alban had become a Christian too.'

'What happened next?'

'The soldiers finally tracked down the only place the Christian could be and it was then that Alban made his fatal move. He disguised himself as the Christian so that the other fellow could get away.

'Well, you can imagine how furious the magistrate was when he found out that his troops had arrested the wrong man. But, to be fair to him, he told Alban he could go free if he apologised and gave up his Christianity there and then.'

'But Alban wouldn't.'

'No, he certainly would not. So, to set an example, the magistrate ordered that he be taken out and executed – and so here we are.'

'Thank you, sir. Well, listeners, you heard that. I am now moving along with this procession and I can tell you there is a very strange feeling in the air. The soldiers don't seem very happy and the crowd are very quiet.

'A few minutes ago we came to the river and it seemed far too deep to cross, yet when Alban stepped into it there was no problem.

'I am afraid the execution is now taking place and . . . and again the strangest things are happening. Several of the soldiers are kneeling down and . . . and hundreds in the crowd are doing the same. I'm going to try and have a word with the man I spoke to before – he's kneeling too.

'Excuse me, sir. Why are people behaving like this?'

'If Christianity can give Alban the courage to behave in the way he did then I want to be a Christian too. I imagine all these other people feel the same way.'

'Thank you. Well, listeners, now you have my report on what happened to Alban. We know from living in our time what an example he set for other Christians. We know too that the town he lived in eventually became St Albans and a magnificent church now stands on the place where these events happened.'

Information for the teacher

1   St Alban's Day is celebrated on 22nd June but details of his life are extremely vague. There are no contemporary records of his life and the first written accounts of him did not appear until at least two hundred years after his death. The date of his death, however, is not fixed with any certainty. Many accounts depict it as 'about 209' but one source has it as late as 303.

2   The various accounts of St Alban's martyrdom are also very disparate. He is credited with 'parting the waters' of the river. One story also said that this feat converted the first executioner to Christianity and a replacement had to be found.

3   This story could be linked with those of others who have suffered for their Christian faith. Included in this group could be other saints and, of course, many Biblical figures. St Paul is one obvious choice, with his journeys and imprisonments, leading up to his execution in AD 65 (Acts 13–28).

Hymn suggestion

Come and Praise Vol 1 'He who would valiant be' No 44

Prayer

Dear God,

Let us pray this morning that we can learn from those people who always behave in the way they believe they should. Let us remember Alban's kindness to the man who was frightened and being chased by others. Let us pray for a world where people are kinder to each other. Amen.

National Curriculum Cross Curricular Reference

This story has considerable dramatic potential and also offers much scope for discussion. The historical link would obviously be with Roman Britain. There is little evidence of these happenings but the period was probably during the reign of the Roman Emperor Diocletian. Art could be involved in reproducing pictures of dress and buildings of the time.

40   This month

Introduction

June is usually one of the loveliest months of the whole year, and one in which there is a great deal to see and do out of doors.

This month

June is a month which writers and poets like to describe. One poem goes like this:

> Full early in the morning
> Awakes the summer sun,
> The month of June arriving,
> The cold and night are done;
> The cuckoo is a fine bird,
> She whistles as she flies,
> And as she whistles 'cuckoo',
> The bluer grow the skies.
> (Anon.)

If you take a walk in fields or woods on a June day you would expect to see lots of flowers. There are pink and white dog roses, and wild hyacinths. Yellow and white daisies are scattered throughout fields and in damp spots there are large, blueish-purple flowers called meadow cranesbill. You might also see flowers which look like large buttercups and these are called marsh marigolds. As well as looking, it is a good idea to take deep breaths and then you might get the lovely smell of honeysuckle, which is a plant which twines round other plants and hedges.

If you go anywhere near a pond, watch out for tadpoles, which by

June have longer legs and shorter tails. Sticklebacks are around and there is certainly lots of activity above the surface of the pond. Watch out for dragonflies, butterflies and moths in the air.

Perhaps the fruit we all think of most, in connection with June, is the strawberry. The Romans called strawberries *fragaria* but our name for them comes from the fact that this is a fruit which spreads long runners over the ground: we say that it 'strews' these, and so they were first called 'streoberries' and eventually 'strawberries'. There's a special way to pick strawberries so that you don't damage them. Each berry should be snapped off with the first finger and thumb, about a quarter of an inch from the berry along its stem. You should always be careful to touch the actual berry as little as possible because this causes it to 'smear', or bruise.

Some birds like berries, of course, and there are plenty of them to see and hear during June. Although the poem we heard earlier mentions the cuckoo, this bird will be heard less than in May. This is because he leaves earlier than others for warmer conditions. So don't expect to hear many cuckoos after about the third week of June. Other birds to watch out for and listen to are hedge-sparrows, blackbirds, goldcrests, chaffinches and linnets.

Finally, if you live in southern England, then listen out at dusk on a calm, quiet June night. You could well hear the whirring noise of stag beetles flying about. If you see one, you can tell if it's male because it will have things that look like antlers, but which are really long jaws.

Information for the teacher

1   James Lowell said, 'What is rare as a day in June?' Practically all the points mentioned in the assembly text can be extended further. For instance, there are more interesting stories relating to strawberries. In earlier times, and for several obvious reasons, they were considered a much greater delicacy than they are today. In consequence highwaymen were very active in waylaying strawberry consignments – not surprising when their rarity brought as much as £10 for 1lb of strawberries in London.

2   There are an unusual number of poems and pieces of prose which could be used with children during June. 'A hot day' by A S J Tessimond is particularly good, with many telling lines ('A tree, June lazy . . .'). Other good choices of poems are 'An Indian Summer on the Prairie' by Vachel Lindsay, 'On a Midsummer's Eve' by Thomas Hardy, and 'Summer' by Christina Rosetti.

  For prose, a dip into Laurie Lee's *Cider with Rosie* is rewarding.

Hymn suggestion

Come and Praise Vol 1 'For the beauty of the earth' No 11

Prayer

Dear God,
Please help us to use our senses to appreciate summer's beauty. Help us not only to enjoy the sights, smells and sounds of the countryside, but to be aware of how important it is to look after it in every way we can. We thank you for the pleasure we get in sharing lovely summer days. Amen.

National Curriculum Cross Curricular Reference

The link with English is obvious via the poems and prose mentioned and there are also obvious opportunities for the children's own descriptive writing. Science and/or Environmental Studies are also well catered for in the 'natural' activity of June and there is unusual scope for Art out of doors.

Musical links with June are about as prolific as the literary ones: 'Waltz of the Flowers' (Tchaikovsky): *Fantasia on Greensleeves* (Vaughan Williams): the Overture to *A Midsummer Night's Dream* (Mendelssohn); and 'Morning' (prelude to Act 4 of *Peer Gynt* by Grieg). Add to these the various popular 'show standards': 'June is bustin' out all over', 'Summertime', 'Oh, what a beautiful morning', etc, and it can be seen that there is a considerable variety of material. The children could be encouraged to improvise some appropriate music of their own.

41 John

Introduction

You all know that if you are going to have a party there has to be a lot of preparation beforehand. It's the same for things like sports days or swimming galas or school trips. This morning's story is about a man who had to prepare people for a great event.

Story

Zacharias was a priest in the temple at Jerusalem in the time before Jesus was born. He and his wife Elisabeth were very excited.

'I wonder if it will be a boy,' muttered Elisabeth to herself as she went about her daily jobs. She and Zacharias had no children so they were looking forward to the birth of their first child.

When the great day arrived, a boy was born and he was called John. Many people thought that when he grew up he would be a priest like his father, but John had other ideas. He was very fit and strong and did a lot of thinking by himself. One day he spoke seriously to his father.

'I must leave home,' he said. 'I feel that the job I have to do in life can't be done here.'

'But where will you go?' asked Zacharias.

'I am going to live in the desert,' replied John. 'There I will get the chance to talk to people who pass by. I feel that I have a lot to say to them.'

So John left Jerusalem and went to live in the desert. He lived alone and life was very hard. Then he began to make regular journeys to the great river which was nearby. This was the River Jordan and many people passed along it every day.

'Listen to me, I have something to tell you,' said John to these people. 'You must try and live better lives than you are doing now.'

'What do you mean?' asked a tax collector who was passing by.

'Well – you, for instance. You collect taxes. Do you ever cheat and take more tax than you should, keeping the extra for yourself?'

The tax collector looked shiftily away.

'Well, if you do, you must stop and live a better, fairer life – being generous to others rather than trying to cheat them.'

'And you, soldier – it is easy for you with your power to treat people badly. But you shouldn't. Remember, someone as strong as you can help people rather than frighten them.'

So John went on talking to the travellers by the River Jordan. Soon he became so well known that people went especially to hear him speak. They asked him questions.

'What can we do to live better lives? Can you help us?'

As well as advising them, John then baptised many people in the waters of the river. He also kept on telling them that a man, much more important than he was, was soon coming to show them how they must live. John's listeners did not know it but the man he was preparing for was Jesus.

Information for the teacher

1 The Bible references for this story are as follows: Luke 1 and Mark 1. Moving on further, the story of Jesus's baptism is in Matthew 3, 16–17; and that of John's death in Mark 6, 27–9.

2 John was supposedly born at a village four miles west of Jerusalem and showed an early predilection for the austere life. Honey was one of his main foods in the desert and he wore a cloak of camel's hair tied with a belt. It was John's regular baptising of people in the Jordan that gave him the name 'John the Baptist'.

   As well as having many listeners, John also attracted some close followers and friends (Matthew 9, 14; Luke 7, 18).

3 The Roman authorities were always apprehensive about potential 'troublemakers' who gathered followers. Herod Antipas considered that John fell into this category and had him arrested. He was subsequently beheaded at the request of Salome.

4 John the Baptist's Day is 24th June. One of his symbols is camel's hair ('And John was clothed with camel's hair, and with a girdle of a skin about his loins', Mark 1, 6). St John the Baptist is the patron saint of Florence.

Hymn suggestion

Come and Praise Vol 1 'The journey of life' No 45

Prayer

Let us pray this morning for those who prepare. Let us give thanks for their work and care, and pray that their preparation is appreciated and rewarded. Amen.

National Curriculum Cross Curricular Reference

Geography could be involved in locating the settings of the story. A link with Science could consider what are people's 'basic needs' to stay alive in a 'wilderness'.

42   *Six wise men?*

Introduction

'I know I'm right!' I'm sure you have heard people say that. Sometimes, though, it is better to listen to another point of view first before being certain that we are right – as this morning's story shows.

Story

The king was fabulously rich.

'I want to use some of my riches to find really wise men,' he said to his courtiers. 'Go and find me six of the so-called wisest men in the kingdom and tell them I want to reward them for their wisdom.'

So six wise men were brought before the king.

'Now,' said the king, 'the wisest among you will be rewarded with a large sum of money – or, if you prove equally wise, the money will be shared between you.'

'Ah,' thought each of the men, 'I'm sure I am wiser than these others. It will just be a question of proving it when the king sets his test.'

'Right,' said the king, clapping his hands and bringing his servants scurrying towards him. 'Get six very large blindfolds and tie them tightly round each of these wise men's heads.'

This was done and then, with a servant leading each of them, the six men were taken outside into the palace gardens. Silently tethered in the garden and, of course unseen by the men, was an elephant.

'This is what we are going to do,' said the king. 'Each of you will be led out to feel something. When you have all felt it you are free to discuss what you think it is – and decide together – or you can make your own choice without discussing it with the others.'

The first wise man was led by his servant up to the elephant. His hands were placed firmly on the elephant's tusk and and he was told not to move them.

'This is a great thick spear,' he thought to himself. 'I don't need to talk to anybody about that. I'm sure I'm right. So I'll get all the money.'

The second man was led up to the elephant and when his hands were placed on the elephant's leg he was positive he was holding a tree. His thoughts about winning everything for himself were exactly the same as the first man's.

The third man was sure he had hold of a rope as he held the

elephant's tail; the fourth believed the elephant's chest was a wall and the fifth thought he had hold of a carpet when the servant put his hands on the creature's ear!

The sixth man was just the same as the rest. When he was lifted to sit briefly on the elephant's back he thought he was on a large covered rock.

When all had had their turns, the king ordered the elephant to be taken away. When this was done the blindfolds were removed and the wise men were asked to tell the king what they had touched.

'A spear, Your Majesty.'

'A tree, Your Majesty.'

As each man said what he thought he had touched, the others could hardly contain their laughter for thinking how stupid their fellow competitors were. When they had all finished the king ordered the elephant to be brought back. As it lumbered into view, the faces of all six men dropped in astonishment. How could they have been so wrong?

'You have all proved your lack of wisdom,' said the king. 'Each of you was so greedy to get all the money for himself that he was sure he was right and didn't want to share his opinion with the others. But if you had discussed what each of you felt you would have realised it was an elephant. Then each of you would have got something – instead, all of you get nothing.'

Information for the teacher

1   This is an adaptation of an old Hindu story. In at least one other version the wise men are competing for the hand of the king's daughter.

2   A useful calendar link for this story could be 27th June. On this date in 1880 Helen Keller was born. She was to lose her sight and hearing completely before she was two, but overcame her difficulties and became well known and admired for her championing of the handicapped.

3   The idea of wisdom being a sharing of knowledge is captured in a quotation from Tolstoy: 'The highest wisdom has but one science – the science of the whole'.

4   A good source for stories of this type is *Faith Stories for Today* by Angela Wood (Longman).

Hymn suggestion

Come and Praise Vol 1 'Join with us' No 30

Prayer

Dear God,
Teach us the value of sharing – our talents, our good fortune, our worries, our disappointments. Help us to learn that by sharing these, and other things, in our lives we become much wiser people. Amen.

National Curriculum Cross Curricular Reference

Words like 'wisdom', 'sharing', and 'unselfishness' in the context of this, and other stories, provide good discussion possibilities. Some work on the senses could incorporate Science, as could a closer look at elephants. There could be scope for some imaginative work in Art in relation to this story.

43   To the rescue

Introduction

You never know when you might suddenly be called upon to make a quick decision – which could be very important. This morning's story is about a schoolboy who had to act very quickly one June day.

Story

This is one of those stories where people are brought together quickly and by accident. It happened one warm day late in June.

'We're just a mile from the main factory,' said helicopter pilot Ken Lynburn to his passengers. They were all in a helicopter belonging to a firm called JCB Excavators.

Hardly had the words left the pilot's mouth than the machine began to shake violently. Something had obviously gone very wrong and the pilot struggled desperately to keep control. As he fought with the controls, the helicopter began to sink earthwards.

Meanwhile, down on the ground, a schoolboy, Andrew Nelson and a student teacher, Steven Morris, heard the uneven noise of the helicopter's failing engine. Looking up, they saw the machine swinging unevenly through the sky – and getting lower all the time.

'It's going to crash!' shouted Andrew.

'You're right,' replied Steven, 'it's going to come down in that cornfield over there. It can't hold up much longer . . . oh my . . .'

There was a terrifying crash as the helicopter ploughed into a cornfield a short distance away. After the racket of the engine and the noise of the rotor blades there was a sudden, ominous and frightening silence.

'Come on!' shouted Andrew. 'We've got to help.'

'But the river . . .' muttered Steven as he followed in the footsteps of the running boy.

'We'll cross it,' gasped Andrew.

The two raced to the banks of the River Dove and, without hesitation, waded straight into it. The water swept up to their waists but, pushing their legs as quickly as they could through it, they soon emerged dripping on the other side.

'There's still no sound from that helicopter,' muttered Steven.

'No – they're obviously all hurt in there – but it's fire I'm worried about,' replied Andrew as the two pounded over the cornfield.

'Yes,' muttered Steven through clenched teeth, thinking of fuel running out of the machine's tanks with the possibility of an explosion and fire at any second.

Andrew was the first to reach the crumpled wreckage. Without hesitation, he forced his way through the mangled door and, faced with a cabin full of unconscious bodies, he scrambled to where the electrical leads were connected to the batteries. With a firm wrench he pulled them out.

'Now there's no danger of a short circuit setting all this fuel on fire,' he muttered to himself as the overpowering smell of escaped fuel made his head swim.

By now Steven had reached the helicopter too, and in the distance other rescuers were running across the field to help. Soon the emergency services had arrived and the injured men were lifted tenderly out of the wreck and taken to hospital.

Without Andrew's quick-thinking, knowledge and speedy action, however, a fire could have started at any time and then no one in the helicopter would have survived.

Information for the teacher

1   This helicopter crash took place near Uttoxeter in Staffordshire.

Andrew Nelson was eighteen and a pupil at nearby Abbotsholme School. The incident occurred on 28th June 1990 and there were six people in the helicopter. Unfortunately two were killed in the crash; the other four were taken to hospital in Stoke-on-Trent.

2   This rescue depended considerably on Andrew's knowledge of the requirements of fire prevention. A useful address in this context is: Fire Protection Association, 140 Aldersgate Street, London EC1A 4HY.

3   The notion of helping others is very strong in all religions. Useful quotations here are:

'Woe to him that is alone when he falleth, for he hath not another to help him up.' (Ecclesiastes 4, 10)

'He is best loved who does most good to other creatures.' (Islamic saying)

'Share each other's troubles and problems.' (Galations 6, 2)

'Be worthy of a reputation.' (Confucius)

Hymn suggestion

Come and Praise Vol 2 'You've got to move' No 107

Prayer

Let us give thanks this morning for the courage, determination, speed and skill with which some people help those in need.

Let us give thanks for the fact that in times of trouble so many people show these qualities. Amen.

National Curriculum Cross Curricular Reference

Science would feature here with work on flight and helicopters in particular. Linked with Technology, this could obviously involve some practical work. Some research into the causes of flight failure might also be undertaken. A look at First Aid could be incorporated in these subjects.

The 'flight' theme could be extended into History with some work on the history of powered flight and helicopter development.

The story has plenty of scope for drama; and an examination of the requirements of moving quickly could involve Physical Education.

44   *You can't make bricks without straw*

Introduction

There are lots of sayings which we use as little reminders. We say: 'More haste, less speed'; 'Don't count your chickens before they're hatched'; 'Look before you leap.' (The Presenter might comment on those.)

This morning's story is about a saying: 'You can't make bricks without straw'.

Story

Moses and Aaron, the leaders of the Hebrews who lived in Egypt, were worried.

'To think we were once honoured guests here,' said Moses.

'Yes,' replied Aaron. 'When Joseph was alive he was the second most important man in the country after the Pharaoh.'

'And now we are just slaves,' Moses went on. 'We must go to the Pharaoh and tell him we want to leave to worship God in the desert.'

So Moses and Aaron went to see the Pharaoh, the king of Egypt, and told him what they wanted for their people. The Pharaoh was furious. If the Hebrew slaves left, his own people would have to do all the hard labour.

'I will not let you leave,' he said to Moses and Aaron. 'In fact, as a punishment for your asking, your people will now have to make all the bricks and collect the straw to go in them.'

Moses and Aaron were astounded: This would make the Hebrews work almost unbearable. For years they had made all the bricks used by the Egyptians, but the Egyptians had collected the straw for them. The Hebrews had gathered mud from the valley of the River Nile, then mixed this mud with chopped straw collected by the Egyptians, and then put the mud and straw mixture into moulds to make bricks.

'The Pharaoh wants us to make the same number of bricks,' said Moses to the people.

'But to do so we will have to work twice as hard because now we have to collect and chop the straw as well,' Aaron continued.

'We must go,' said the people.

'Yes, we'll have to leave, no matter what.'

Then the Egyptians will have to do everything themselves.'

So the Hebrews decided then and there that they must leave Egypt. Later, with God's help, they did. His foolish judgement finally cost the Pharaoh all his workers.

Information for the teacher

1   The Biblical reference for this famous incident is Exodus 5, 10: 'Thus saith Pharaoh, "I will not give you straw. Go yourselves, get your straw wherever you can find it; but your work will not be lessened in the least." '

2   Further discussion can take place on the folly of trying to complete something without an essential ingredient. In this context, without the scattering of straw in the brick moulds it was almost impossible to turn them cleanly and cut them free when they were dry.

3   The idea of sage advice derived from sayings could be followed up with more examples.

4   The story ends with the brief phrase that eventually the Hebrews left Egypt. This of course is a long and dramatic story in itself and for teachers who want to use it the Biblical reference is Exodus 5–14.

5   As this story contains the point which led the Hebrews to seek and gain independence, it could be linked to several other Independence anniversaries which take place this month. For instance, 4th July is the date on which the USA celebrates its Declaration of Independence in 1776. Other countries which celebrate similar occasions during the month are Venezuela (1811) and Algeria (1962) on 5th July; Argentina (1816) on 9th July; Belgium (1831) on 21st July.

Hymn suggestion

Come and Praise Vol 2 'What about being old Moses?' No 81

Prayer

Let us think this morning about how important it is to have all the right qualities to be a complete person. Let us remember that it is not enough to be kind and thoughtful just some of the time. Let us learn to be always reliable.

National Curriculum Cross Curricular Reference

History, Geography and RE could all be interwoven in the stories of the Hebrews in Egypt and their escape from it. There is plenty of scope for drama too. A wider historical sweep might incorporate the freedom of slaves on a worldwide basis; and 'songs of slavery' could be a valuable musical accompaniment here. Technology could involve some practical, simple brick-making.

45   Rich as Rockefeller

Introduction

If somebody has a lot of money an old saying claims that they are as 'rich as Rockefeller'. This is because John D Rockefeller was one of the richest men the world has ever known – but he was also one of the kindest.

Story

'It's a boy!' William Rockefeller looked at the newborn baby in his wife Eliza's arms and shouted with delight.
   'Yes,' smiled Eliza, 'let's call him John.'
   The date was 8th July 1839 and the Rockefellers lived in a small village near New York in the United States of America.
   When John was a young man, the family moved to Cleveland and he borrowed some money from his father to set up a business selling salt and meat. From that moment on John moved into more and more businesses and made more and more money. He started to refine oil, he bought forests so that he could use the timber to make barrels, he made paints, paraffin and dyes.
   'It seems that no matter what I do, I make money,' thought John to himself, 'so I must help others who don't have enough.'
   So John continued to give away money – something he had done since he was a very young man with very little of his own. He gave money to universities in Chicago, London, Oxford, Edinburgh and Bristol. He paid for a foundation which worked to cure terrible

diseases in the world, like malaria and yellow fever. He rescued Mexico from starvation when all its crops failed, and helped people all over the world as different as farmers and ballet dancers.

To have some idea of what sort of man John Rockefeller was, however, is to remember something that happened in Cleveland when he was a young man. At this time many people in America, whose ancestors had been brought from Africa, were still slaves. One day a man came to see John.

'Sir,' said the man, 'some friends of mine have told me that you are against slavery – and that you are a very kind man.'

'Well,' replied John, 'I don't think that any human being should be a slave for another human being. As for being kind – it's nice of you to say so, but I just try to give a little help where I can.'

'I have come to you for help, sir,' the man went on. 'Because I lost my job I couldn't pay a debt. As a result my wife was taken away from me and made a slave to the person to whom I owe money. I can only get her back and free if . . .'

John held up his hand. 'Say no more, my friend,' he said. 'Just tell me how much you need.'

Information for the teacher

1   John D Rockefeller was born in 1839 and died in 1937, aged ninety-seven. Nobody has ever been able to calculate just how much money he gave away – but to Chicago University alone he gave one hundred million pounds during his lifetime. While being an incredible philanthropist, he live very frugally and worked hard.

2   The adaptation of some words from Ecclesiasticus 4 are very appropriate for use with the life of Rockefeller: 'Don't refuse to help the poor, deny the hungry, be mean to those who need money and avoid people you think poorer than you.'

   There are other useful quotations along the same themes: 'Give all you can' (John Wesley); 'Give and do not count the cost' (St Ignatius); 'What really counts is man' (Ghanian proverb); and 'Be worthy of a reputation' (Confucius).

3   For those who want to extend this theme, two other men could be linked with Rockefeller. John Wellcome was an American who became a British subject in 1910. Immensely wealthy, he created the Wellcome Foundation which gives financial help to every form of medical research. He died on 26th July 1936.

   William Morris (Lord Nuffield) made a fortune from can manufacture and formed the Nuffield Foundation with a gift of ten million pounds. He once put a cheque for £100,000 in a Red Cross collection box. He died in August 1963.

Hymn suggestion

Come and Praise Vol 2 'Bread for the world' No 75

Prayer

Dear God,
We give thanks this morning for those people who can always find time and effort to help others. Amen.

National Curriculum Cross Curricular Reference

Geography could be involved in locating New York and Cleveland; the history of oil development could be linked with scientific work to give a better understanding of refining and its byproducts. 'Money' is a theme which could obviously have mathematical links.

46   The traveller's gift

Introduction

This morning we hear first about a lovely idea – and then the strange story which started it off.

Story

For many years travellers on the Pacific Ocean have practised a thoughtful custom. Whenever they are making a sea journey they throw coconuts overboard. The story which follows tells how this custom came about.

Sina was a beautiful girl who lived on one of the islands in the Pacific. One day she was walking near a pool on the island when she saw a huge eel swimming in it. Going nearer to the pool she was astonished when the eel suddenly changed into a handsome young man.

'Do not be frightened of me, Sina,' said the young man. 'I am the protector of all eels, but I so much wanted to talk to you that I changed myself into human form.'

Sina was astonished to hear this, but soon she and the young man became great friends. At their meetings he changed into a human being, and when she left he went back to being an eel.

Then one day the young man had some very sad news. 'I am going to leave this place,' he said, 'and I will never see you again. I would like to give you a wonderful present before I go, so this is what you must do.'

The young man then told Sina exactly what she had to do during the next day.

Well, next day, because of what the young man had said to her, Sina was not surprised when a terrible storm broke out. The river bubbled and surged up out of the valley and, sitting in her house on the hill, Sina watched the water get higher and higher. Then, out of the water, leapt an eel which landed on Sina's doorstep.

Remembering her instructions, Sina immediately cut off the eel's head and buried it on the hillside near her house. The flood water went down and every day after that the beautiful girl went to look at the spot where the eel's head was buried.

Time passed and then she noticed a tall green shoot growing. Soon it grew more strongly until eventually it was a magnificent tree. Then it came into flower and finally large bunches of nuts hung from the branches.

Sina and all her family and friends were delighted with the tree. It was indeed a wonderful present – the coconuts not only provided food, but drink as well; the leaves could be woven to make mats and canoe sails, and could be used to thatch huts.

So the custom came about. Anybody sailing from one island to another in the Pacific threw a coconut overboard. This was because they thought it was a wonderful present which might save the life of a shipwrecked sailor, or reach another island and start to grow there.

Information for the teacher

1   There are a few collections of stories from the South Pacific and one of the very best is *Tales from the South Pacific Islands* by Anne Gittins (Stemmer House). Mrs Gittins was the wife of a colonial administrator and tells the stories with a verve and charm which make them compulsive reading – and often very useful for assemblies.

2   This idea of 'help for the traveller' is a strongly held Islamic tradition; Muhammad's concern for beasts of transport such as camels is illustrated by several stories. Christianity has a patron

saint of travellers (St Christopher) and the Bible is full of stories of journeys where help is needed: Jacob (Genesis 27–35); Joseph (Genesis 37–45); the crossing of the Red Sea (Exodus 14, 21–2); the Promised Land (Joshua 6); the good Samaritan (Luke 10); and St Paul's journey (Acts 13–28).

3   There are some useful travel anniversaries which can be linked to this story. On 8th July 1978 Naomi James completed her journey having sailed round the world single-handed; on the 16th, in 1963 Valentina Tereshkova, as the first woman in space, circled the earth in her space craft *Vostok 6*; on the 22nd in 1964 Sir Francis Chichester set a new record for sailing single-handed across the Atlantic in under thirty days.

Hymn suggestion

Come and Praise Vol 1 'Travel on' No 42

Prayer

Let us give thanks this morning for all those who by their care, thoughtfulness, concern and wisdom help all who travel by sea, air or land. Amen.

National Curriculum Cross Curricular Reference

Geography could be involved in locating the South Pacific and finding out more details of the islands there – their climate, vegetation, population etc. Science could be involved in finding out more about coconuts; a History link could be with the development of sea travel. There are possibilities for unusual and dramatic work in Art, and Technology might be involved in looking at some of the activities of making sails, weaving, etc.

47   Be prepared

Introduction

This morning's story has a very simple message: Be prepared!

Story

It was a glorious summer's day in July. The sun shone down brightly and a few wispy clouds drifted lazily by in a deep blue haze. The countryside was peaceful and still – well, almost still.

'Gosh, this is warm work, but it will certainly be worth it eventually.'

This was an ant speaking. He didn't really have too much time for speaking because he was working too hard. Backwards and forwards he scurried, collecting grains of wheat and then stacking them away in a hole. All round him, his friends were busy on the same job.

Now it happened that a grasshopper had been watching the ant who had spoken.

'Hey, you!' called out the grasshopper.

'Are you speaking to me?' asked the ant, as he hurried on another journey.

'Look at me for a minute,' said the grasshopper.

The ant shot him a quick look. 'Well?'

'You see what I'm doing, don't you,' went on the grasshopper. 'I'm doing nothing. I'm sitting here enjoying the sun – doing absolutely nothing – and it's great.'

'Good for you,' replied the ant. 'But if I did nothing now I'd pay for it later.'

'What do you mean?' asked the grasshopper.

'If you don't know that, then you're sillier than I thought,' said the ant. 'Now, if you'll excuse me, I've got work to do. Then I can sit and do nothing.'

So the day went by, the grasshopper basking in the sun, the ant working hard. The next day was very similar, and the next . . . but as the weeks went by the weather began to change. The sky clouded over, a cold wind began to cut through the trees, rain fell, and then flurries of snow came down. Winter had arrived.

Warm and contented in his home the ant ate the food he had collected in the summer and waited patiently for the weather to change again. One day he had a visitor.

'I've called to see you,' said the grasshopper.

The ant looked at his visitor. Gone was the confident creature who had poked fun at him back in July for working. Now the grasshopper was shaking with cold and looked and sounded very miserable.

'It's nice of you to visit me,' said the ant, 'but what is it you want?'

'Food!' cried the grasshopper. 'All that food you stacked away in the summer. I can't get any and I'm starving. Please let me have some of your food.'

'I'm sorry,' said the ant, 'but I've just been checking my supplies and I've got just enough to see me through the winter. You should have thought about this in the summer when all you wanted to do was enjoy yourself.'

Information for the teacher

1   This is one of those old tales which can be adapted and to feature different creatures or people. It can also be very easily dramatised and used in this form in an assembly preparation.

2   The most popular Biblical story in the 'Be prepared' theme is that which tells of the girls at a wedding. Five of the ten girls took spare oil so that their lamps would be certain to stay lit when the bridegroom arrived. Five didn't bother, and consequently their lamps went out and they couldn't borrow any more oil.

Hymn suggestion

Come and Praise   Vol 1 'Give me oil in my lamp'   No 43

Prayer

Dear God,
Please help us to help ourselves. Give us the wisdom to take care and make preparations, and not to rely on other people to get out of difficulties which have come about through our own carelessness. Amen.

National Curriculum Cross Curricular Reference

This is the sort of story which can promote discussion and the telling and writing of stories with a similar message. A scientific bias could involve examining the effects of winter on animals, their needs during this time, and how they use the summer to prepare for these needs.

Some interesting improvised music might be created as background to this story. A sharp contrast could be expressed between the indolent, relaxed grasshopper and the busy, mobile ant.

48   One of Scotland's Brave

Introduction

This morning's story is about a man whose bravery and determination saved the lives of every single person who was on a ship with him. This is Jim Maxwell's story.

Story

'Isn't it beautiful?'

'Look at that scenery.'

'Oh, I *am* looking forward to this trip.'

The passengers strolled round the deck of the ship pointing out the sights to each other. It was a beautiful July evening in 1827 and the ship, the *Clydesdale* had just left Scotland on its journey to Ireland.

As darkness fell, the passengers went below to their cabins to enjoy a good night's rest. Captain Turner paced the bridge, and the pilot, Jim Maxwell, stood at the wheel, guiding the ship through the night.

It was when the ship was about halfway on its journey that both captain and pilot became aware of a familiar and terrifying smell.

'Something's burning,' said Captain Turner.

'You're right, Skipper,' replied Maxwell.

'Keep her on course for Ireland,' ordered the captain, and went in search of the smell.

He didn't have to look very far. When he reached the top of the engine room ladder, he not only felt a blast of hot air but he also saw the first flames begin to burn the starboard side of the ship.

'Emergency!' bellowed the captain at the top of his voice. Within seconds, every member of the crew was at work fighting the flames with buckets of water. The passengers were alerted and rushed on deck to the fore part of the ship, where the flames were least likely to reach them.

'We're in desperate trouble,' thought Captain Turner. 'Our only hope is speed. If we can reach land before the boilers blow up or we're burnt to death, we have a chance.'

Now, unknown to Captain Turner, Jim Maxwell had disobeyed orders. Thinking that they would have a better chance of beaching on the familiar coasts of Scotland, he had steered the ship round on a course for home.

So began a nightmare journey. More and more of the ship was on fire despite the crew's non-stop efforts to beat back the flames. The engines became white hot with the strain the terrific speed imposed upon them, and the passengers grew more and more terrified.

The calmest man on board was Jim Maxwell. The soles of his feet began to blister with the heat coming from below decks, black smoke billowed around him, almost choking him, and his clothes began to singe as the flames licked upwards.

'Leave the wheel, man! Lash it on the course we want and get up on deck.'

Captain Turner shouted this not once but three times to the brave pilot.

'No, we need a man at the wheel to guide us in,' replied Jim.

Finally, the ship began to blaze around him and the wheel in his hands started to char and singe.

'Get some water on him,' shouted the captain.

So a chain of sailors began to pass buckets of water, and the last one threw each bucket of freezing water over the pilot's smouldering clothes. Still he held on, burnt hands gripping the wheel as bucket after bucket of water crashed over him, keeping the roaring flames back for a few seconds each time.

'Land!' cried one of the passengers suddenly. 'Land! Land!'

Sure enough, the familiar outline of the Scottish coast came clearly into view as the doomed ship raced ahead. A huge crowd on the shore gasped in horror as the floating inferno surged towards them.

'They'll never make it.'

'She'll blow up any second.'

'I wonder how many have died already?'

With his eyes fixed firmly on the coast ahead Jim steered the ship towards a shallow beach. Then, with a screaming of timber on the stony shore, the bows of the *Clydesdale* ground to a sudden stop. At once the people on the shore rushed to help the terrified passengers and exhausted crew. Jim Maxwell was found slumped unconscious over his burning wheel, and tender hands rushed him ashore and to hospital.

After some weeks there, he made a full recovery and returned to his work on ships. Thanks to his courage and determination not a single life had been lost on the *Clydesdale*, and he had become one of the most famous men in Scotland.

'Just doing my job,' was all this modest, brave man would say about the night he steered the blazing ship to safety.

Information for the teacher

1 The *Clydesdale* was bound for the west coast of Ireland, having just left the Clyde, when this incident occurred. When Jim Maxwell's story became known a public subscription was opened for him.
2 Useful addresses are: Royal National Lifeboat Institution, West Quay Road, Poole, Dorset B15 1HZ; and the Fire Protection Association, 140 Aldersgate Street, London EC1A 4HY.

Hymn suggestion

Come and Praise Vol 1 'A man for all people' No 27

Prayer

Let us think this morning about the courage of people like Jim Maxwell. Let us remember, too, the support people need in difficult situations. Give us the strength to be always someone who will 'lend a hand'.

National Curriculum Cross Curricular Reference

'Fire' is a subject well suited to areas as diverse as poetry and painting. Musically it could be supported by the very appropriate 'Fire Down Below', and Falla's *Ritual Fire Dance*.

   Both ships and fire could be involved in Science and Technology work.

49 *This month*

Introduction

July is a good month for using our senses of sight, smell, hearing and touch out of doors. There is plenty to look at – but you may need to listen a bit more carefully.

Story

There is a sense of peace about the countryside in July. The excitement and activity of spring is over and things seem to be relaxing before preparing for autumn.

Birds are a lot quieter. By the middle of the month the cuckoo will have left for warmer climates and birds like song thrushes and song warblers won't be singing any more. Sparrows are still likely to be noisy and fussy and can be seen swarming round cornfields.

There are, however, other noises to listen out for, although careful listening is necessary. You are not likely to hear the scuffling of field mice and moles, but you may hear the squeaking of shrews hunting about for insects in the woods. This is the time when bats are about at night, too.

The hot weather brings out lizards, which dodge about looking for spiders and flies. Grass snakes are about near ponds, looking for food like frogs and newts. On the drier ground of heath and moor adders lie out in the sun. They are easily recognised by the zigzag markings on their backs and they should be left well alone!

There are hundreds of flowers in bloom in July. Watch out particularly for the light-blue heads of scabious, which look like pincushions; the blue nettleflowers which looks like wild Canterbury bells; the tall pink rosebay willow herb and the wild clematis which grows over hedges.

Keep an eye out too for butterflies – the purple hairstreak, warbled white and the rarer but beautiful purple emperor. At night there is the magic of tiny pricks of light which show that glow worms are about.

Another of the senses you will use in July is the feel of heat and humidity, and of the sudden threat of heavy rain. If you are caught in a thunderstorm, remember to check how far away from you its centre is. To do this, start counting the seconds between the flash of lightning and the clap of thunder. Every five seconds equals one mile.

Information for the teacher

1   July was the month of Julius Caesar's birth. The Anglo-Saxons called it 'Hey Monath' – the time of hay harvesting.
2   Rain and storms are significant in connection with St. Swithin's Day on the 15th, but there are other notable 'wet' happenings in the month, too. The Spanish Armada which was seen approaching England on 19th July 1588, was almost totally devastated by a tremendous storm after its clash with the English fleet. In 1945 a

freak storm off Resguill, County Donegal, deposited shoals of fish in the streets!

Nevertheless, rain was a valued commodity in rural England:

> A shower of rain in July
> When the corn begins to fill,
> Is worth a plough of oxen,
> And all belongs these till.

Hymn suggestion

Come and Praise Vol 1 'For the beauty of the earth' No 11

Prayer

Dear God,
We thank you for giving us the beauty of the world around us, and the senses with which we can enjoy it. Amen.

National Curriculum Cross Curricular Reference

In a Geography/Science link a great deal could be made of any 'water' aspect of July. For instance, a chart containing the Beaufort notation could be displayed and kept up to date. The relevant symbols for use are: bc – sky half covered with cloud; c – cloudy; d -drizzle; e – wet air; f – fog (visibility between 200 and 1,000 metres; F – thick fog (visibility less than 200 metres); g – gloom; L – lightning; o – overcast sky; p – squalls; r – rain; R – heavy rain; t – thunder.

The uses and value of water could also be discussed. A suitable musical addition would be 'Dance of the Spirits of Water' by Gustav Holst.

50 What can I do to help?

Introduction

Have you ever noticed how often we make excuses about things? 'I'm too busy to do that . . . What good could I do? . . . I'm not clever enough to do that . . . ' and so on. This morning's story is about a man who used his time, energy and talents to help others.

Story

It was a summer's evening and the man was watching a programme on television. He was comfortable and well fed, but the children he saw on the television screen were starving and crying. They were living in a country called Ethiopia, where the weather was so dry that families couldn't grow enough crops to keep themselves alive.

'These people need help,' thought the man to himself, 'and there must be thousands of others like them who also need help. Now what can I do that would be useful?'

This man was a musician so, with some friends, he wrote a song. Then he got some more friends to help him make a record of the song. By the time all this had happened it was getting near to Christmas.

This was just what the man wanted because the song was called 'Do they know it's Christmas?' and he hoped lots of people would buy the record. He was right. The song told of the suffering of people in Africa and it sold millions of copies all over the world.

'Now I must use the money to help those starving children,' thought the man. So he started a fund called Band Aid and he went to Africa himself to see how the money was being used to help.

'Well, it's certainly helping,' thought the man, 'but they need so much! I must organise something else to get more money to help.'

This time he had a brilliant idea. What if he held a huge pop concert, got lots of stars to sing and play at it – and then used all the profits to help those desperate people in Africa? Better still – what if he held *two* pop concerts . . .

So the man started to work really hard again. He hired Wembley Stadium in London, and the John F Kennedy Stadium in Philadelphia, USA. Between them these two stadiums could hold a hundred and sixty thousand people! Next he started to organise the groups and stars to sing at the concerts, and finally he booked the date – 13th July.

'I must think of a special name for these concerts,' thought the man. 'I think a good name could be . . . Live Aid.'

So the two huge concerts were held. Each stadium was packed and the events were broadcast throughout the world. As well as the singing, the huge screens showed scenes from Africa when there was a pause in the music. The whole thing was a tremendous success and the staggering sum of forty million pounds was raised.

With this money the man got ships to take food to Africa and lorries to carry it further, right to where it was needed most. Thanks to him, thousands and thousands of lives were saved. The man's name was Bob Geldof.

Information for the teacher

1   Bob Geldof started this work in 1984. The Live Aid concerts were held on 13th July 1985. His further work included a cookery book (the *Food Aid Cookery Book*) and Sport Aid (May 1986) which included many sponsored running events.

2   One common link between major religious figures is the help they gave to others. This assembly book, and the *Autumn* and *Spring* assembly books in the same series give examples in the stories about Jesus, Muhammad, the Buddha, Guru Nanak and other lesser figures.

3   Several useful quotations can be used in advocating help for others and making sure that we are not 'insensible to other men's needs' (Job).

   'Don't refuse to help the poor . . . deny the hungry . . . be mean to those who need money.' (Adapted from Ecclesiasticus 4)

   'He is best loved who does most good to other creatures.' (Islamic proverb)

   'Give a man a fish and you feed him for a day. Teach a man to fish and you feed him for life.' (Confucius)

   'Let us learn to give and not to count the cost.' (St Ignatius)

4   In view of the titles of the organisations inspired by Bob Geldof a definition of 'Aid' may be useful: 'to render assistance to; promote the success of; assist; help; succour'. (Funk and Wagnall)

5   A useful parallel to this story could be the work of Mother Teresa. Born in Yugoslavia in 1910, she went to India in 1948 to be a teacher. She was so shocked by conditions there that she has spent the rest of her life seeking to improve them. Her 'Prayer for Peace' has been translated into over four hundred languages, and in 1979 she was awarded the Nobel Peace Prize. Gifts of money and medicine are sent from throughout the world to help her mission.

Hymn suggestion

Come and Praise Vol 2 'Bread for the world' No 75

Prayer

Let us give thanks this morning for the energy and determination of people like Bob Geldof who, when they see a need, do something about it.

National Curriculum Cross Curricular Reference

Science and Geography are closely interwoven in looking at why some areas of the world pose more threat of starvation than others. A look at the basic needs of the human body could be compared with the local difficulties in seeing that these can always be met.

Maths and Technology could be linked in examining the simple logistics involved in getting aid over the seas and into a country like Africa. The link with Music is an obvious one; and there is a great deal of discussion potential here, too.

51   Stick together!

Introduction

This morning's story reminds us that we all need friends. If we choose to be the sort of person who is disagreeable and unfriendly then we might find ourselves alone. Once we are alone, well . . . listen to the story.

Story

The lion stood looking down at the field which lay baking in the sun. How hungry he felt! Even more so as he looked at the four well-fed bulls who grazed in the field.

'All I've got to do is to get one of them away from the others – and I've got my dinner!' thought the lion.

Stealthily he crept down to the field. Soon he was in position to leap onto one of the bulls. At that moment, however, one of the other bulls saw the lion, gave a loud snort and galloped over. He was quickly followed by the other two bulls.

The lion snarled in dismay. As long as the four bulls were grouped together like this, he couldn't attack. He would have to go hungry. But he was a patient animal.

Finding what food he could elsewhere, he returned to the field every day to look at the bulls.

Meanwhile, the bulls kept a look out for each other and grouped together at the first sign of trouble. That is, until the day they had the argument.

Nobody could remember how it started, but it ended with the bulls no longer speaking to each other and storming off – each one to a corner of the field.

This was just the opportunity the lion had been waiting for. That night he killed one of the bulls and by the end of the week he had killed them all.

'How could those bulls have been so foolish?' he thought to himself as he stared down at the now empty field.

Information for the teacher

1   This adaptation of the well-known fable by Aesop could be used as a starting point to link with several others which not only have a 'message', but also have the lion as a central character. Any collection of Aesop's fables – *Aesop's Fables*, retold by Ann McGovern, (Scholastic) is a good one – will probably contain stories such as 'The donkey in the lion's skin'; 'The man and the lion'; 'The stag at the pool'; 'The donkey, the rooster and the lion'; 'The lion and the boar'; 'The wolf, the lion and the lamb'; 'The lion and the mouse'and 'The sick lion'.

2   The lion is a very significant creature in Biblical writings. Although now extinct there, lions were common in the Jordan Valley of Old Testament times, and were also found in the mountains of Judea and Samaria.

   They were infamous for killing men (I Kings 13,24) and sheep (I Samuel 17,34). It was a tribute to a man's courage and strength to kill a lion (Judges 14,5; I Samuel 17, 34–7). The famous story of Daniel in the lion's den is in Daniel 6, 16–23.

   Artists have used the lion to symbolise St Mark. Perhaps this is because his gospel is 'the voice of one crying in the wilderness'. Old Testament writers regularly wrote about the roar of the lion in the country around.

Hymn suggestion

Come and Praise Vol 2 'All the animals' No 80

Prayer

Let us think this morning about how much we can learn from stories. So many stories have been written by wise people with a lot to teach us. Let us learn to be good listeners.

National Curriculum Cross Curricular Reference

'Stories with messages' is a theme which could embrace both English and RE. The location of current lion habitats would be a useful geographical exercise and Science could be involved in finding out why they have become extinct in some areas, why they flourish in others, what are their needs, habits, habitats, etc. History could be involved in looking at the significance of lions in the past – Samson, Daniel, St Jerome and the lion, Richard the Lionheart, etc.

52 Rumours

Introduction

Sometimes, particularly when people get excited, they say things which they are not certain are true. They say them as if they were, though – and that's how 'rumours' start.

Story

The hare was a very nervous creature, always fearing the worst.

'I wonder what dreadful thing is going to happen today?' he said to himself one morning. 'What a worry life is! What's that?'

Just beyond the bushes where he was crouching there was a heavy, soft thud.

'It's the . . . it's the earth falling in! The end of the world! The earth is falling in!'

Racing off as fast as he could, the hare fled. He hadn't gone very far before he bumped into a deer – another nervous creature.

'What is it?' asked the deer anxiously.

'Run!' said the hare. 'There's danger everywhere . . . it's the earth . . .'

At once the deer started running in panic. When he reached a pack of buffalo he called out. 'Hurry, run for your lives!'

Hearing the panic in the deer's voice, the buffaloes thought it would be better to be safe than sorry. They started to pick up speed in a dusty gallop.

Everywhere the rumour spread: danger – run for your life. Boars, tigers, even elephants moved uneasily and quickly in the hare's path.

Eventually the rumour reached the lion. When he heard that everything had started with the hare he set out to find him.

'Now look here,' said the lion when he had stopped the running animals, 'tell me exactly what happened.'

'The earth,' gasped the hare, 'is breaking up. I heard it. we must get away!'

'What did you hear?' went on the lion.

'A terrible thud – terrible – just like the earth breaking.'

Well, the lion continued to question the hare until he decided that he had heard enough.

'Right,' he said, 'Now get on my back and take me to exactly where this happened. You other animals – I want you to wait here until we get back.'

The huge crowd of animals shifted about nervously while the lion ran back to the clump of bushes where it had all started. The hare, clinging to his back, was terrified. Eventually they reached the bushes – and there, lying on the ground, was a huge, heavy fruit. It had fallen behind the bushes where the hare had been sitting.

'There,' said the lion, 'that's what you heard – that heavy fruit falling to the ground.'

The hare looked down shamefacedly. 'I'm . . . I'm sorry for all the trouble I caused,' he said.

'Well, I think you've learned a lesson,' went on the lion. 'Now you've got to go back and tell the other animals exactly what happened.'

Information for the teacher

1   In this old story the lion supposedly represents the Buddha who had been reborn in this new guise to give the sort of advice to the animal world which he had already given to humans.

2   The idea of rumours and the confusion they can generate is one which can be readily followed up with children as they have an almost innate grasp of this subject! This can lead on to a more serious consideration of telling the truth, particularly in the context of human relationships, and although this is a story with a Buddhist background an African proverb is a useful reminder here:

>   A word is like water.
>   Once spilled it cannot be gathered again.

3   At the time of writing the Buddhist festival of Dhammacacka falls in July. (Its regular location is the full moon day of the Buddhist month of Asalha.) This is a good calendar link with the story

because it celebrates the Buddha's first sermon.

Hymn suggestion

Come and Praise Vol.2. 'A still small voice' No 96

Prayer

Dear God,
Help us to remember how much harm we can do by using the wrong
words. Teach us to speak with truth, kindness and consideration so
that what we say never causes any trouble or hurt to anyone else.
Amen.

National Curriculum Cross Curricular Reference

This is a theme which lends itself to much discussion – and dramatic
work – in English. Geography could be involved in locating countries
where Buddhism is most prevalent. There seems scope for some
dramatic Art work linked to this particular story, with collage and
three-dimensional work special possibilities.

53   Locked in

Introduction

This morning's story is a true one which happened a few years ago.
None of the people in the story is famous and what happened might
well have happened to you some time.

Story

It was a usual sort of morning for the Simpson family. Dad was eating
his breakfast quickly before going to work; Mum was feeding baby Sue
and three-year-old Paul was whizzing his cars about the floor.

The family lived in a bungalow in a hot country and all the windows
and doors were wide open to let in some breeze.

Paul suddenly stood up and walked down the corridor to the
bathroom. Nobody else paid much attention – not even when they
heard the click of the bolt being locked on the other side of the door.

Everybody paid attention about five minutes later, however . . .

'Help! I'm locked in!'

Paul's voice carried from the bathroom, along with sounds of banging on the door.

'Oh no,' said Mum, hurrying down the corridor. 'Push the bolt back, Paul – push it with your fingers.'

'I can't, Mum. I've tried and tried but I can't move it.'

'Well keep trying – push hard.'

By now Dad had left the breakfast table and joined Mum outside the bathroom door.

'He's never going to be able to move that bolt.'

'Well what can we do? This door's as solid as a rock.'

'I'll have to go round and get in through the window.'

Now, this wasn't as easy as it sounds. Although the window was obviously on the ground floor because the building was a bungalow, it was covered by a huge steel grill. This was to keep burglars out when the windows were left open at night.

'You'll be late for work, Geoff,' Mum called out to Dad.

'No, I won't. Anyway, we can't leave him in there all day!'

'No!' cried a tearful voice from the bathroom.

So Dad got his tools out and began to take out the screws which held the massive steel frame in place. Ten minutes later he eased the frame down onto the ground, and hauled himself up, through the window, and into the bathroom.

'Hello, Dad,' said Paul with a pleased smile.

Information for the teacher

1   This incident took place in Singapore before air conditioning was commonplace.

2   The main theme which could be developed from this story is one of feeling safe and protected in the care of those who love us. Minor problems are just that when family help is at hand.

3   An appropriate Shakespearean quotation might be: 'It is a wise father that knows his own child.' (*The Merchant of Venice*)

Hymn suggestion

Come and Praise Vol 2 'When your Father' No 73

Prayer

Dear God,
We thank you this morning for those who care for us, who help us in difficulty and protect us when we are young. Amen.

National Curriculum Cross Curricular Reference

This is ideal starting material to provoke first-hand stories from children about 'adventures' with their parents, grandparents, brothers, sisters, etc. These could be talked about and written and could also give rise to some good dramatic possibilities.

The practical aspects of the story – removing screws, frames, etc. could be linked with Science and/or Technology activities.

54   Team work

Introduction

Sometimes, in a difficult situation, it is impossible for one person to put things right – but a little help from somebody else makes all the difference.

Story

'What a magnificent day.'

So thought Lieutenant Tristram of the Fleet Air Arm as he sat at the controls of his Scimitar fighter plane three thousand feet above the glittering blue water of the Mediterranean Sea. To his right flew the plane of his friend Sub-Lieutenant Bosworth.

At a speed of 520 miles per hour the planes cut through the clear blue sky as they circled the south coast of Crete. They had both taken off earlier from the aircraft carrier HMS *Hermes*.

'What a magnificent—'

Lieutenant Tristram was just about to say the same thing again when there was a sudden tremendous explosion in front of his face. Momentarily blinded, he felt the outside air screaming and tearing round his face. Within seconds he realised what had happened – a bird had flown into the windscreen of the plane. The force of this had broken the windscreen, injured his face and made it almost impossible for him to see anything. Thoughts raced through Lieutenant Tristram's mind . . .

'I can't see . . . I must get out . . . I must fire my ejector seat . . . but can I save this valuable aircraft? I must try . . .'

Desperately the injured pilot sent out an emergency Mayday call to his fellow pilot, Lieutenant Bosworth. Back came an encouraging reply.

'Your plane is flying straight and level. There doesn't seem to be anything wrong with it. What do you want to do?'

'Thanks,' said Lieutenant Tristram. 'Give me radio instructions on how to get back to the ship and we'll see what happens then.'

So began a nerve-racking flight. Buffeted by the howling wind, and barely able to see anything, Lieutenant Tristram flew his plane according to the instructions given to him over the radio by Lieutenant Bosworth.

'Nearly home,' said Lieutenant Bosworth eventually. 'The aircraft carrier is in sight down below. Why don't you bail out now and I'll radio them to send out a boat to pick you up?'

'No – thanks all the same,' said Lieutenant Tristram. 'I've got this far and I'm going to try to land. After all, there's nothing wrong with this plane other than a broken windscreen.'

Slowing his aircraft down to its minimum flying speed, and peering desperately through the broken windscreen, Lieutenant Tristram could see the aircraft carrier in a blur in front of him.

'You're nearly down – but you're too high,' came the voice of Lieutenant Bosworth in his headphones.

Lieutenant Tristram prepared to fly round again, but suddenly, out of the side window of his plane, he saw how near he was to the flight deck. Making an instant decision, he cut his engine, and the plane sank to the deck and was caught safely by the arrestor wires which stretched across the deck.

Minutes later Lieutenant Bosworth landed and the two pilots – and their aeroplanes – were back safe and sound.

Information for the teacher

1 This incident took place in July 1962. Lieutenant Tristram ultimately received the Queen's Commendation for Bravery in the Air.

2 The 'Mayday' aspect of this story could be followed up by

reference to the origins of this call sign, which is told in the May assembly, 'Mayday' (page 58).

3 Two addresses which could be useful in connection with this story are:

Amateur Radio Society of Great Britain, Alma House, Cranborne Road, Potters Bar, Herts. (This is a society of radio amateurs and short wave listeners.)

Navy Records Society, c/o Royal Naval College, Greenwich, London SE10 9NN.

Hymn suggestion

Come and Praise Vol 1 'We are climbing' No 49

Prayer

Dear God,
Let us pray this morning for those people who are involved in accidents. Let us give thanks for those who are trained to help, and those who show courage, determination and quick-thinking.

Let us pray for the safety of all those people who are today making journeys on land, on the sea, or in the air. Amen.

National Curriculum Cross Curricular Reference

Science and Technology could certainly be involved in a number of ways here: flight – by machine and bird, glass – strength and weakness; impacts, etc. The location of the story would be a useful geographical exercise and the history of aircraft carriers could trace their development, difficulties, etc.

55   *The Sultan's gift*

Introduction

Have you noticed how really kind people always have time – to listen to problems, to help out where they can, to give advice if it is asked for? This morning's story is about such a man.

Story

Abdul was desperate. After years of struggling to keep themselves alive, he and his wife now had nothing left.

'There's only one thing to do,' said Mehnaz, Abdul's wife, 'we'll have to ask for help.'

'But we've lived out here in the desert all our lives,' replied Abdul. 'Nobody out here has anything either. Who can we ask who is not desperately poor too?'

'We must ask the richest man we know of – the sultan of the great city.'

'Ha,' said Abdul. 'You must be mad! Why should the Sultan listen to a nobody like me?'

'I've heard he is a kind and fair man,' said Mehnaz. 'After all, we have nothing to lose. No . . . you must go and see him and take him a gift of the best thing we can offer.'

Abdul didn't need to ask what this was. Everybody who lived in the desert looked upon water as the most precious thing there was. So Abdul took a cup of their precious water supply, covered it tightly with a cloth and set out on the long journey to the city.

For several days the old man travelled. Desperate for food, his ragged clothing barely enough to keep off the hot sun, he was almost exhausted when he reached the city. As one who had lived all his life in the country he was amazed at the sights and sounds of the great city.

Finally, he came to the sultan's palace – and there he saw a sight which horrified him. Running through the gardens outside the palace banks on either side of it was – a river! The water looked clear and fresh and bubbled over the stones in the riverbed.

'Water,' gasped Abdul. 'Water – gallons and gallons of it, clear and fresh and plentiful. How can my pitiful little cup of ditchwater be any good now? I may as well go straight back home and give up.'

Now one of the sultan's servants had been watching Abdul, and seeing what a poor state he was in, he came up to the old man.

'Can I help you?' he said kindly.

'Oh – you startled me,' replied Abdul. 'No, I don't think you can, thanks. You see, I came to see the sultan. I brought him a gift and I wanted to ask his help . . . ' Abdul's voice tailed off as he looked miserably down at the pathetic covered cup in his hand. The servant, seeing that the old man was at the end of his tether, put an arm round his shoulders and said, 'Come with me.'

A few minutes later Abdul stood in front of the sultan. All the things he had been going to say had vanished from his head. He felt an old fool. The sultan smiled.

'Many people come to see me, my friend, but my servant tells me you have come a very long way and have brought a gift.'

Still unable to speak Abdul shamefacedly held out the cup, covered with its old and dusty cloth. A servant took it, cut away the cloth and handed it to the sultan.

Without a moment's pause the sultan lifted the cup to his mouth and drank every drop of water. When he had done so he smacked his lips and held up the cup in his hand.

'Wonderful!' he said. 'That is some of the very best water I have ever tasted. It must have been very precious to you – and I thank you for letting me have some. Now, one gift deserves another. Servant – fill this cup with jewels, cover it carefully and then see that my friend here is escorted through the city on his way home.'

Abdul managed to stutter a Thank You to the sultan and then he found himself once more outside the palace. He couldn't get over the sultan's thoughtfulness and kindness.

'For a man to value such a small gift that he didn't even need, and to reward it with such kindness . . . that surely is a great man.'

Information for the teacher

1 This story is an adaptation of an Islamic one from a thirteenth-century writer called Sumi.
2 As water features so strongly in this story it could be linked with one of Christianity's most famous July anniversaries. This is St Swithin's Day on 15th July. St Swithin, Bishop of Winchester and renowned for his humility and kindness, died in 862 and, at his request, was buried in the churchyard. In 891 a group of monks felt that it was inappropriate for such a distinguished man to languish outside the church so, on 15th July of that year, they set about removing his remains to put them inside the church. Torrential rain began immediately, and continued for forty days – until the remains were returned to the churchyard grave.

Hymn suggestion

Come and Praise Vol 2 'It's the spring' No 82

Prayer

Dear God,
We thank you this morning for the kindness of so many people: those
who listen to us when we are in difficulties and for whom it is never too
much trouble to help in any way they can. Amen.

National Curriculum Cross Curricular Reference

This is a story which could provide many possibilities for drama,
discussion and creative writing. From a scientific point of view, 'water'
and 'deserts' are two subjects offering considerable interest which
could be linked with Geography. History could be involved in more
research into the time when St Swithin was alive. The transport of
water, in small or large quantities, could involve Technology. There
are plenty of musical associations, including Handel's *Water Music*,
Holst's 'Dance of the Spirits of Water', Debussy's *La Mer*, and
popular standards such as 'Singin' in the Rain', and 'Cool Water'.

56   Enough for everybody

Introduction

The end of the summer term in school is an exciting time. There are
sports days and class outings and everybody looks forward to these.
This morning's story is about a class trip.

Story

'It's going to be great.'
    'All those trees that we can climb after the picnic.' 'And there's a
boating lake too . . .'
    '. . . and Miss Jennings says we can get boats out if we like.'
    Class 5 was full of excitement. It was the morning of the class trip.
The register had been called, the coach was waiting at the end of the
lane and Mrs Waters and Mrs Brown, the ancillary helpers, had taken
all the picnic stuff along already.
    'All right, get in twos and calm down.'

Miss Jennings looked completely different in her jeans and with her hair tied back in a ponytail – but Class 5 still knew when it was time to stop messing about.

Half an hour later, the coach was cruising along the motorway heading for Marefield Forest. The sun glinted through the windows, nobody felt sick and in ten minutes they would be there!

Sure enough the coach pulled into the carpark right on time. There was only one other coach there.

'Right,' said Miss Jennings. 'Now, every group has got two hours to do their activity. Those who are going boating will be with Mrs Waters; the Nature Trail people are with Mrs Brown.'

Miss Jennings went on briskly to tell everybody where they would be and who they would be with.

'At exactly twelve o'clock,' she said finally, 'everybody will come back to the little clearing which is marked on your maps. There is never anybody there so we'll have the place to ourselves for our splendid picnic.'

There was a great cheer when she said this.

Well, it was a fantastic morning. Geoff Wall tore a hole in his trousers climbing a tree, Emma Bywaters lost a shoe in the lake and Sertan Uhal found a box of ten horseshoes buried near a tree.

At twelve o'clock everybody was hungry and the leaders headed their groups back to the marked clearing. Then there was an unpleasant surprise.

'Somebody else is there.'

'It's those kids from that other school.'

'Miss Jennings said nobody else ever came here.'

'They've pinched our spot.'

'It's not fair.'

Class 5 were unhappy. They stood on the edge of the clearing watching the other schoolchildren taking all the best spots and unpacking their picnic boxes. It just wasn't fair!

Miss Jennings had just arrived and was about to speak to them when suddenly the coach driver came up and pushed his way through to her. He looked very worried.

'Is there something wrong?' asked Miss Jennings.

'Well . . . not exactly wrong,' said the coach driver, 'But you know your two ladies brought that big hamper with all the picnic stuff along the lane for me to put on the coach . . . '

'Yes,' said Miss Jennings, in an apprehensive voice.

'Well . . . I didn't.'

'You mean . . . '

'We've got no food – it's still standing on the pavement back near the school.'

It was at that moment that a teacher from the other school came up to Miss Jennings.

'I'm sorry to butt in,' he said, 'but I couldn't help overhearing and . . . we'd be very pleased to share what we have with you. Wouldn't we, kids?' he suddenly shouted to all the other children who were just about to start eating.

'YES!' came a great shout back.

Well, within five minutes Miss Jennings and this teacher had got things organised. Class 5 was split into groups and each group joined some of the children from the other school. You know what it's like in school outings – and parties: there's always too much food, so there was plenty to go round.

What's more, everybody made new friends. Miss Jennings and the teacher from the other school seemed to get on very well together, and it was great.

'Best school trip I've ever been on,' said Sertan later in the afternoon.

'You bet,' replied Geoff, 'and to think when we first saw those other kids we didn't like them.'

Information for the teacher

1   There are obvious twin themes here – one of sharing, and the other of judging people before we know them. This story could be presented in assembly by having one child read it, while the others in the class act it out.

2   All religions advocate generosity to those less fortunate. Some useful quotations are:

'Be forebearing with one another and charitable.' (Ephesians 4,2)

'A kind word counts for more than a rich present; With a generous man you will find both.' (Ecclesiasticus 18, 16–17)

3   Obviously July is an ideal month to present this assembly and its presentation could be linked to some class outing.

Hymn suggestion

Come and Praise Vol 2 'Bread for the world' No 75

Prayer

Let us think this morning about some words spoken by a famous saint. These words are: 'Let us learn to give and not to count the cost.' Amen.

(From a prayer of St Ignatius)

National Curriculum Cross Curricular Reference

This story seems most suited to discussion, drama and the consideration of other stories of generosity, hasty judgements, etc. Physical Education might be linked in considering some of the physical activities possible during an outing to a forest.

57   *The traveller's friend*

Introduction

Often we need determination to complete a task which seems very difficult. But 'sticking at something' often brings its own reward, as this morning's story reminds us . . .

Story

The river was deep and fast-flowing and the man who sat on a stone on its banks was tall, strong and broad shouldered.

'That Christopher,' people used to say about him, 'I reckon he could carry an elephant across that river!'

They were exaggerating, of course, but they were talking about Christopher's job. This was to carry people from one side of the river to the other. There was no bridge so Christopher sat there and waited for travellers who needed to cross. Then, taking them on his back he strode out into the water and delivered them, mostly dry, to the other side.

Well, one day Christopher was sitting on his usual stone when he heard a voice behind.

'Would you take me across, please, sir?'

Christopher looked round and saw a small boy standing there. 'Certainly young man,' he said, 'Come on, hop onto my back.'

'This is an easy one,' thought Christopher to himself, 'this lad is as light as a feather – I wish they were all like this.'

So saying, the ferryman stepped into the fast-moving water and, feeling his feet crunch on the familiar stones, set off for the other side. It must have been when he was nearly halfway across that he felt the weight on his back suddenly begin to get heavier . . . and heavier.

'I can't . . . I can't understand it,' he gasped.

The weight was now almost unbearable. Christopher felt as if his legs were being forced down into the river bed. Sweat poured down his face and he gritted his teeth with the enormous effort he was making.

Finally, with the last drain of his strength, Christopher reached the other side of the river and collapsed exhausted onto the bank. Unable to understand what had happened, he heard the child's voice speaking to him.

'You have done well, my friend. My name is Jesus, and, you see, you were not only carrying me but the weight of all things people do wrong in the world as well. You don't need telling what a terrible weight that is.'

Information for the teacher

1   St Christopher's Day is 25th July and he died on this day sometime in the third century. He was supposedly a man of immense strength – 'twelve cubits in length' – and after this episode left the river to be baptised and become a Christian. He was martyred for his faith during the reign of the Emperor Decius.
2   St Christopher is the patron saint of travellers. A famous woodcutting depicting the incident of the story, and dating from 1423, has inscribed on it that whoever views the picture will be safe for the day.

Hymn suggestion

Come and Praise Vol 1 'Travel on' No 42

Prayer

Dear God,
Let us pray this morning for all those who are about to set off on journeys. May they be protected from all dangers and arrive safely at their destinations. Amen.

National Curriculum Cross Curricular Reference

A link with Science and/or Technology would be created by further consideration of how rivers might be crossed. This could incorporate rafts, boats and bridges and include some quite far-reaching practical work. History could also be involved in examining the timescale for the developments of these things. The story has dramatic possibilities and Art could be involved in looking at some of the many depictions of St Christopher (on medals, etc) which can be found relatively easily.

58   *Underground treasure*

Introduction

This morning's story is about how a man used his senses as well as he could. This helped him to hear, and see, something which not only changed his own life, but saved many other people's lives as well.

Story

Cadoc was a young man who lived high up in the Welsh mountains. What he wanted more than anything else in life was to be able to read the Bible. This was difficult because at that time all Bibles were written in Latin, and nobody in the mountains knew anything about Latin. Then one day Cadoc heard some good news.

'There's a holy man come to live in a village in the valley,' said one of Cadoc's friends. 'If you go down and live there perhaps he will teach you how to read the Bible.'

So Cadoc made the long journey to the village. He found the holy man, explained what he wanted and said he would do any work to help in the village.

'Ah, I'm sorry, my boy,' said the holy man, 'but it's impossible. You see, we've no food in the valley. There might, with a struggle, be enough to keep most of us alive through the winter, but we cannot feed another mouth. You must leave at once.'

Cadoc was bitterly disappointed. Not only did he realise that he couldn't take any of the desperately needed food, but he also wished that he could find some way of helping the unfortunate people.

'There must be something I can do to help,' he thought to himself.

So he went and sat on a tree stump just outside the village. It was a beautiful July day. The sun shone from a cloudless sky and the trees cast long shadows around the thoughtful young man.

Bowing his head, Cadoc prayed, and concentrated for all he was worth. Then, he heard a tiny noise on the ground near him. Keeping absolutely still, he moved only his eyes to see where it had come from. The noise came again and this time Cadoc spotted its source. A tiny mouse was edging out from some bushes. Glancing nervously from side to side, it then dashed to a hole in a nearby tree.

It was gone in a flash but even this short time had been enough for Cadoc to see that it had been carrying a grain of wheat in its mouth.

'That mouse is obviously building a store of food for the winter,' he thought. 'But as everybody is starving here and the crops have failed – where is it getting the wheat from?'

Cadoc knew he must find out. Searching in his pocket, he found a piece of thread. Then he crouched down beside the hole and waited for the mouse to reappear. When it did, he grabbed it firmly but gently, and tied the thread round its body. Then, with a stroke, he released the tiny creature.

Unwinding the thread as the mouse ran off to the bushes, Cadoc followed carefully. When he had parted the bushes and come to the clearing on the other side, he was just in time to see the mouse disappearing down a crack in a pile of stones. He waited patiently and, sure enough, it returned shortly with another wheat grain in its mouth.

Cadoc waited no longer. Pausing only to remember carefully the exact position of the stones, he dashed back into the village.

'Quick, quick,' he gasped to the first person he saw. 'Get some men together, with picks and spades. I think I've found some food.'

There was terrific excitement as the group followed Cadoc back to the pile of stones. Then, digging furiously, they began to burrow beneath the pile. In a very short time they came to a trapdoor, leading down to a cellar.

'I remember now,' said one man who was older than the rest. 'There used to be a cottage which stood here. It fell down some time ago – and this must be its cellar.'

Impatiently, the group broke into the cellar – and there they discovered something which made them hug each other with joy. Sacks and sacks of corn were stacked along the walls of the cellar. There was enough to feed the whole village for months – and then plenty to sow in the spring for next year's crops.

'Well, my boy,' said the holy man when Cadoc returned to the village. 'We can never thank you enough. Now you are very welcome to stay and I will teach you all I can.'

Cadoc proved to be not only a good scholar, but a good man. Soon his fame for helping other people spread far and wide, and a church was built on the spot where the mouse had revealed the cellar.

Information for the teacher

1   Cadoc is a Welsh saint who lived in the sixth century. (His feast day is on 25th September.) Cadoc's desire to learn to read the Bible was motivated by the fact that he believed that if we are without knowledge we literally 'know nothing': 'Without knowledge – no power, no wisdom, no freedom, no beauty, no nobility, no victory, no honour, no "God".'

2   Another version of this story can be found in Dorothy Prescott's book *More Stories for Infants at Home and School* (Blandford). This is an excellent source for varied assembly material.

Hymn suggestion

Come and Praise Vol 2 'Give us hope, Lord' No 87

Prayer

Dear God,
Teach us to use our senses well at all times so that no matter how difficult a problem may be we use all the powers you have given us to try and find a solution. Amen.

National Curriculum Cross Curricular Reference

Some interesting Science work could be done in researching the processes involved in transforming wheat from a grain into our daily food. This story lends itself well to drama and, possibly, some interesting Art as well. Some Physical Education could be involved in considering movements necessary to dig and burrow. Technology could also be involved in considering the best implements with which to dig in various terrains.

59   *All alone*

Introduction

It is always good to have a friend to call upon when you are worried or in trouble. Sometimes, however, we have to face frightening situations by ourselves. William Rankin did.

Story

The jet fighter flew smoothly through the sky high above South
Carolina in the United States of America. At the controls, Lieutenant
Colonel William Rankin glanced at the plane flying alongside and
lifted his hand to wave to the pilot. Bringing his eyes back to the
instruments in the cockpit, he got a very unpleasant shock.

'That's . . . that's the fire-warning light!' he muttered as he saw the
red light winking in front of him. At once the plane started to shudder
and shake and William thought he could smell burning.

'I've got to get out while I can,' he thought.

Quickly calling up his companion on the radio, he prepared to leave
the aircraft, which had in those few moments become almost
uncontrollable.

'Here we go!'

Pulling the lever to operate his ejector seat, he found himself being
flung upwards out of the plane at terrific speed. The shock of the
incredibly cold air after the warmth of his cockpit almost took his
breath away. Then he began tumbling earthwards.

'It's a good job I've got an automatic parachute,' he thought. 'I
know it will open when I reach ten thousand feet above the ground.'

Then William saw something which sent a chill of fear through his
already freezing and battered body. He was falling right into the
middle of a gigantic black thundercloud.

Just before he reached it, the canopy of his parachute cracked open
– and then he was plunged into the rolling blackness of the cloud.
Claps of thunder rocketed against his eardrums and flashes of lightning
seared past his body. Then, to his horror . . .

'I'm going up again!'

Caught in a great current of air sweeping upwards, William found
himself above the cloud again! What followed was a nightmare – one
minute he was plunging downwards, then he was soaring up. All the
time he was in and out of darkness and the noise roared round him.

'My parachute will never survive this,' shouted William aloud. 'It's
bound to tear or fold up. It's . . . '

Then, as suddenly as the horror had started, it was over. He broke
through the bottom of the cloud, the noise and wind stopped, and
there, drifting towards him, were the welcoming green fields below.

Information for the teacher

1   William Rankin was the first man to eject at a speed of 500 mph
    and a height of 47,000 feet. The temperature outside his aircraft

was seventy degrees below zero. His descent to the ground should have taken ten minutes, but such was the turbulence that it took him forty minutes finally to reach land.

2 This incident took place on 29th July 1959 and Rankin was a Lieutenant Colonel in the United States Marine Corps.

Hymn suggestion

Come and Praise Vol 1 'He who would valiant be' No 44

Prayer

Dear God,
We ask this morning that we may be given the courage to face difficulties and disappointments when there is no one but You to help us. Please give us the strength to be brave and determined. Amen.

National Curriculum Cross Curricular Reference

This story abounds with scientific opportunities. Extremes of weather and their causes is one; powered flight is another. Technology could be linked with Science in some practical experiments with parachutes – always a popular topic with primary children.

Geography could be involved in locating South Carolina; the history of powered flight is another possible area for research. This story could promote some interesting creative writing – being frightened, darkness, feelings of falling, etc. An interesting musical exercise might be to select and listen to some music which portrays first the violence of the fall, then the tranquillity – perhaps Mussorgsky's *Night on the Bare Mountain* followed by a quiet passage from Rimsky-Korsakov's *Scheherezade*.

60   The pattern

Introduction

All our lives have a pattern to them, but it is what we do which often helps to decide what the pattern is. In July many eleven-year-old children leave their junior schools for the last time, ready to go to secondary schools in the autumn. This is part of life's pattern.

Story

Wayne was fed up.

'I don't want to leave Brookfield,' he said. 'I like it here and I don't want to go to that big secondary school in Charters Lane. It's a dump.'

None of the others in Mr Haine's class bothered much when Wayne said this. Although they all liked him, he wasn't very good at much. They were all looking forward to French, and better Science, a zippy uniform . . . and maybe a bit of homework.

'It'll be great, Wayne.'

'We can't play rugby at this school.'

'I hear the drama club is really good there,' said Debbie Clark who happened to hear what they were talking about.

'Hmm,' muttered Wayne.

Now, although Wayne wasn't good at much at school, he did try hard and he knew what he wanted to be.

'Just like Dad – that's what,' he would say to himself.

Mr Dawkins, Wayne's Dad, was a motor mechanic and Wayne used to watch for hours as his stubby fingers changed starter motors, adjusted points and cleaned oil filters.

'Hello Wayne,' said Mrs Dawkins when her son got home that afternoon.

'Hello, Mum. Where's Dad?'

'Need you ask?'

Wayne grinned. Dad was rebuilding an old Morris Minor in the garage at the bottom of the garden. Every spare minute he was down there.

When Wayne got to the garage his dad was bent over the re-built engine of the car. The bonnet was up and he was making some fine adjustment.

'Hello, son.'

'Dad, I don't want to go to the secondary school. It's a dump and they reckon there are bullies there and . . . '

Mr Dawkins straightened up and wiped his hands with an oily rag.

'Come here, son,' he said. 'Now look at this engine – there are the new plugs I've put in, the fan belt is tightened perfectly, the carburettor is cleaned out, there's petrol in the tank – but as it is at the moment the whole thing is no good to anybody. Now watch.'

Mr Dawkins squeezed past Wayne and got into the driver's seat. With a twist of the ignition key, he started the engine, and then came back and stood beside his son. They looked at the engine which had now come to life. It throbbed and the parts moved efficiently.

'See what I mean?' said Dad, but Wayne looked puzzled. 'An engine's a bit like a life – all the parts are there, but until they're working smoothly together it's no good. Going to secondary school is a bit like that. It's a part we have to do – and do as well as we can – and then it goes towards making our lives run like this engine is doing.'

Wayne felt his Dad give him a gentle punch on the shoulder. He had never thought about it like that. Suddenly he felt completely different. Of course he wanted to go to secondary school – how could he ever be a motor mechanic if he didn't?

Information for the teacher

1 This story is obviously end-of-term material with a bias towards those children who will be leaving the school at this time.
2 Two useful quotations might be:
    'Idle hands make a man poor; busy hands grow rich.' (Proverbs 10, 4)
    'One man wins success by his words; another gets his due reward by the work of his hands.' (Proverbs 12, 14)

Hymn suggestion

Come and Praise Vol 1 'The journey of life' No 45

Prayer

Let us pray this morning for all those who will be going to new schools in September. Let us hope that they find friendship and opportunity there and enjoy and benefit from both. Amen.

National Curriculum Cross Curricular Reference

This assembly would provide an opportunity for discussion about the curriculum challenges of the secondary school. It could provide a chance for teachers to reassure children, and stimulate enthusiasm for the future.

Section B
Class Assemblies

This section contains a group of fully-prepared *celebratory class assemblies*. There are suggestions linking them to significant times in the term.

Each assembly is detailed in terms of aims, materials required, calendar location, numbers involved, preparation, information and presentation.

Where there are playscripts for direct use with the children, these are provided in bigger print and can be used for photocopying.

One of the general aims of this section is to produce a detailed resource which requires the minimum of preparation but provides for dramatic and thought-provoking assemblies.

1 Let's celebrate

Aim: Starting with May Day, and leading on to comments on other celebrations, this assembly focuses on the importance of 'giving thanks' and celebrating together.

Materials required: These are very much at the teacher's discretion. One option is to include a maypole and to have children ready prepared to dance round it. Another option is to have the children taking part as Christian, Muslim, Jew, Buddhist, Sikh and Hindu dressed in costume, and/or to carry pictures or artefacts or to perform mimes to illustrate the points they make in each of their monologues.

Numbers involved: Whole class participation

Calendar location: May

Information and Preparation: There is scope for endless adaptation of this assembly and some or all of it could be held out-of-doors. The religious celebrations are only a very small selection of what could be used, but the aim has been to make them topical to the summer term. For more detail on celebrations like these, a very useful source of reference is *Festivals and Celebrations* by Rowland Purton (Simon and Schuster).

The poem 'Lord, touch our careless eyes' is by A C Benson (1862–1925).

Presentation

The introductory music should be something suitably evocative of the theme of May Day and celebrations in general. Depending on availability and teacher/children's preference, this could be any of the following: music for Morris dancing, a march (suggesting the labour aspect of the day), country dancing music, a tape or record of bells ringing, a really good choir singing a hymn, a piece like Clarke's *Trumpet Voluntary* or Grainger's *Shepherd's Hey*.

When the audience is settled and the presenting class is in position, the assembly could begin with four speakers making an introduction.

SPEAKER 1: This morning our assembly starts with some thoughts and information about May Day.

SPEAKER 2: Yes – did you know that in days gone by young people got up very early on May Day? About one o'clock in the morning in fact.

SPEAKER 3: They went to the woods to get branches and flowers and then sang carols as they brought these home.

SPEAKER 4: Young ladies washed their faces in morning dew because they thought this would give them a beautiful complexion.

SPEAKER 1: During May there were many processions and lots of dancing.

SPEAKER 2: Some of the dancing was round a maypole.

(The presenters could now show a model of a maypole; or do a specially prepared dance round one.)

SPEAKER 3: What people were really celebrating on those May Days of the past was the passing of winter and the new life of spring, with the new hopes it brought.

SPEAKER 4: Here is a poem about this:

> Lord, touch our careless eyes;
> New life, new ardour bring,
> That we may read Thy mysteries,
> The wonder of Thy spring.'

SPEAKER 1: When people began to move from the country to live and work in towns, May Day became a time of celebration for the work and labour they did. Great parades took place in towns.

SPEAKER 2: May Day celebrations still start early in the day. At Oxford University the choir of Magdalen College meet at 6 o'clock in the morning to greet the sunrise of the day by singing the May Hymn.

SPEAKER 3: May Day is a day of celebration.

SPEAKER 4: But what is celebration?

At this point the speakers are submerged by the rest of the presenting class who move forward and 'engulf' them. This will of course have been carefully rehearsed beforehand, as will the 'conversational' type comments which will be said aloud by the mingling crowd. These will be said very distinctly so as to be quite audible to the audience:

—Celebrations are festivals, really.

—Yes it's a time when everybody has fun.

—Nobody gets left out.

—It's the sharing of the fun which makes it so good.

—Yes. People remember the good times.

—And in a way they are looking forward as well.

—You're right – hoping for more good times to come.

—I think everybody enjoys some kind of celebration and festivals, don't they?

—I'm sure they do.

—It would be good to find out some of the different ways people enjoy all sorts of celebrations.

At this point the 'crowd' moves back, leaving six children standing at the front. These are: CHRISTIAN, MUSLIM, JEW, BUDDHIST, SIKH and HINDU. They take it in turn to speak as follows.

CHRISTIAN: I am a Christian and we have several celebrations during the year. One of them is Christmas, when we celebrate the birth of Jesus, and another is Easter, when we celebrate his rising from the dead. During the summer term we celebrate Whitsuntide, when, as buds and blossoms open, we remember how the disciples began their work of telling the world about Jesus.

MUSLIM: I am a Muslim. We have a great celebration at the end of the month-long fast we call Ramadan. When the fasting is over, it is Eid-ul-Fitr and we have lots of special food, wear new clothes and exchange cards and presents.

'Happy Eid' is a time when we try to forget all quarrels, make new starts and remember in our prayers those who are not as fortunate as ourselves.

JEW: I am a Jew and one of my favourite celebrations takes place during the summer term. This is Shavuot, when all our synagogues are decorated with plants, fruits and flowers. At home we eat loaves which are decorated with ladders, and *blintzes* which are fritters stuffed with cheese, apple or meat. This festival celebrates Moses receiving the Ten Commandments on Mount Sinai.

BUDDHIST: I am a Buddhist and very early in the summer term we celebrate Wesak. At this festival we celebrate the

Buddha's life. Our houses are decorated with flowers and lanterns, there are long processions, and we exchange presents. One of the best things that happens is that captive birds are set free in memory of the Buddha's kindness.

SIKH: I am a Sikh and in the spring we celebrate Baisakhi, when we remember the great leader Guru Gobind Sing. At this celebration our holy book – the Guru Granth Sahib – is specially decorated, put on a float and carried in a great procession. There is music too, and after the procession everybody crowds into the *langar* (which is our name for kitchen) and has a great meal.

HINDU: I am a Hindu and one of my favourite celebrations takes place after the summer term is ended, during the summer holidays. This is Raksha Bandhan when we think about how important it is to belong to a loving family. On this day all sisters tie a red and gold thread round their brother's wrists. They then pray that this will protect their brothers from all harm. In return the brothers promise always to look after their sisters.

At this stage in the assembly the teacher could focus on what has gone before with the following words:

TEACHER: This morning we have thought about how important celebrations are in our lives. They are times when we give thanks and enjoy the company of other people.

Let us remember the words of the old prayer: 'I have but one journey through the world during my life. Let me use it to be cheerful and kind to others and never put off until tomorrow what I can do today.'

The assembly could end with everybody singing 'Let the world rejoice together' (*Come and Praise* Vol 2 No 148).

2   Travelling along

Aim: To stimulate thought about journeys – through life as well as over distances; a link with the Muslim *Hajj* is incorporated.

Materials required: 'Travel' artefacts such as a suitcase, tickets, labels, passports, travel posters, holiday clothes. Two large pieces of white cloth (eg, white sheets) for 'Rachid'.

Numbers involved: Whole class participation

Calendar location: The summer term – check religious calendars for the dates of the *Hajj*.

Information and preparation: Preparation for this assembly is very basic. For further information about Muslim festivals, a useful book is *Dates and Meanings of Religious and other Festivals* by Dr John Walshe (Foulsham). Not only does it contain more information about the *Hajj* but it also shows how the date of the festival can be worked out each year against the Gregorian calendar.

Help from the Muslim community, or a picture reference, will be needed on how to dress 'Rachid'.

Presentation

The introductory music is important in setting the scene. It should be music evoking travel or movement, and which gives a feeling of journeys and/or holidays. There is plenty of choice here: 'Coronation Scot', 'Chattanooga Choo Choo', 'Summer Holiday', 'Stagecoach', etc.

A set piece of objects should also be in place so that the audience can look at these as they enter, as well as hearing the music, and link the two. Included in the set piece could be suitcases, hold-alls, tickets, labels, passports, travel posters, bathing costumes and holiday clothes.

The assembly could then be started by all the presenting class taking up positions behind the set piece, while the two speakers get proceedings under way.

SPEAKER 1: As you've probably guessed, we're going to talk about journeys this morning.

SPEAKER 2: Journeys at this time of the year often mean family holidays.

SPEAKER 1: Nobody sets off on a journey like that without making proper preparations.

SPEAKER 2: The Bywaters family are getting ready to make a journey to a caravan.

SPEAKER 1: They are going there for a holiday.

SPEAKER 2: Let's take a peep to see what's happening . . .

At this point the action switches to a corner of the presenting area where the 'Bywaters family' can be seen preparing for their journey. DAD, FLOELLA and ANDREW are seen packing. MUM and JULIE are 'off stage'.

DAD: Right, you three – I want to see that you have packed properly.

ANDREW: Toothpaste, soap, towel, pyjamas, trainers, swimming trunks . . .

FLOELLA: Paper, pens, clean clothes, shoe polish, pocket money . . .

DAD: Just a minute, where's Julie? She was here a minute ago.

ANDREW: She's gone out to help Mum pack the car.

FLOELLA: Says she has to help Mum check the air in the tyres, put water in the windscreen washers and see that there's enough oil in the engine.

DAD: I suppose she'll do all that – and then she'll forget her own jeans!

ANDREW: What about you, Dad? What have you got to pack?

DAD: Oh, let's see . . . well, apart from my clothes and things . . . there's cornflakes, washing-up liquid, tinned ham, tomato sauce, frozen butter, milk, eggs and stuff in the cool box, sausages, two cakes . . .

FLOELLA: Stop, stop, Dad – you're making me dizzy!

DAD: Well, when you go away for a week like we're doing you've got to prepare properly. Got to think about home, too – the cat to Aunt Maud's, milk and papers to cancel, Mrs Jackson to come in and water the plants . . . Oh hello, you two!

MUM: Julie and I are off down to the garage. We need a spare fanbelt and a set of plugs and we've got to get filled up with petrol.

JULIE: More oil needed too, Mum.

FLOELLA *and* ANDREW *(together):* Is it worth it?

DAD: You'll only know that when we get there – and when we've got back. Wait and see!

At this stage the action switches back to the two speakers.

SPEAKER 1: You know, all that made me think.

SPEAKER 2: Really?

SPEAKER 1: Yes – our lives are a bit like journeys, aren't they? We start off tiny and as we go along we get bigger and look different . . .

SPEAKER 2: . . . and we learn to do more, and meet more people, and then we grow up and . . .

SPEAKER 1: . . . when we're adults we may have children of our own and it all starts again.

SPEAKER 2: Yes. And, you know, some people make a very special journey because they think that what they learn on this journey can help them to be wiser, better people.

SPEAKER 1: So – let's meet Rachid.

At this stage RACHID *emerges from behind some curtains or screens. He is dressed in two white sheets. One is wrapped round his wrist, the other draped over the left shoulder.*

RACHID: Hello, I'm Rachid. I'm a Muslim and I'm wearing Ihram.

SPEAKER 1: What's that, Rachid?

Rachid: It's what Muslim men wear when they go on the Hajj – which is a pilgrimage to Mecca.

SPEAKER 2: Can you tell us something about Mecca?

RACHID: Yes, it's a holy city for Muslims. Every Muslim tries to make a journey there once in his or her lifetime. Thousands and thousands of people come from all over the world.

SPEAKER 1: What happens there?

RACHID: Well, we wear simple clothes, go to the great mosque and make all sorts of different, smaller journeys to holy places. We make many new friends – and when we go home we feel we are rather special.

SPEAKER 2: How do you mean?

RACHID: Well, we take back holy water, dates and blessings for everyone – which means we can share our great experience with those we left behind.

SPEAKER 1: Thank you, Rachid.

(Rachid leaves the scene.)

SPEAKER 2: So you see we learn so much on journeys – particularly the journey of our own life. Let's all sing together now.

At this stage presenters and audience could join in singing 'The journey of life' (*Come and Praise* Vol 1 No 45). When the singing is ended the teacher could end the service with a prayer:

Let us pray this morning for our journeys through life. May we have the strength to recover from disappointments, the courage to withstand illnesses, the good sense to share our joys and successes. Amen.

3   *From the rough to the smooth*

Aim: To stimulate thought about how we develop as people; about those who help us do so; about the importance of guidance.

Materials required: some rough stones, some smooth stones, candles. *Come and Praise* Vol 1 (No 32, 'Thank you, Lord').

Numbers involved: Whole class participation and a teacher either to play or organise the music at beginning and end

Calendar location: During the second half of the summer term

Information and preparation: The comments which the six children (Child 1', etc) make in this assembly have in some cases been left blank so that in preparing the assembly they can tell their teacher what details and achievements they wish to fill in. The gaps refer to these details:

(*1) eg, 'kicked a football' (appropriate school sport)
(*2) location of a recent school journey
(*3) name of appropriate teacher
(*4) sport, eg, 'football'
(*5) number of goals or points, eg, 'twelve goals'
(*6) any further sporting achievement
(*7) number of months or years
(*8) any celebration particular to the school
(*9) appropriate regional town or city
(*10) (as appropriate)
(*11) (same as *2)
(*12) number of pupils on the trip
(*13) teacher in charge
(*14) any things pupils saw and did

The comments refer to basic school achievements and common interests and can be further adapted as required.

The music could be prepared and played in various ways:
(a) played by a teacher;
(b) played by a small group, with, at the beginning of the assembly, someone to indicate the moments they should break off and start again;
(c) specially recorded in advance.

Presentation

As the audience enter the hall the introductory music should be particularly noticeable in that the piece is constantly being stopped part-way through and started again from the beginning. The presentation begins with two speakers and six other children. When all the audience are in the hall the first speaker could comment about the music.

SPEAKER 1: Did you notice something about our music this morning? (*Pause for responses.*) We never gave it a chance to finish. It was an unfinished piece of music.

SPEAKER 2: Some of our class are now going to come amongst you and give out some stones.

(*Members of the presenting class move among the audience and pass out to the children a good selection of very rough stones.*)

SPEAKER 1: You will notice something about the stones we have given out.

SPEAKER 2: They are very rough and 'unfinished'.

SPEAKER 1: Now feel the next lot of stones.

(*Class members distribute another selection of stones – this time none of them is rough and all are smooth and rounded*).

SPEAKER 2: These stones are a bit like us . . .

SPEAKER 1: We come to school very rough and unprepared . . .

SPEAKER 2: And when we leave we are smoother and don't have the rough, unprepared feel we had when we started.

SPEAKER 1: But how does this happen?

SPEAKER 2: Listen to what some of our class have to say about it . . .

CHILD 1: When I started school I couldn't read and I had no friends to come to school with.

CHILD 2: When I started school I'd never (*1) _____ and I didn't know if I'd be any good at it.

CHILD 3: When I started school I didn't know what a choir was.

CHILD 4: When I started school I had never seen anything called a recorder.

CHILD 5: When I started school I didn't know what a computer was.

CHILD 6: When I started I didn't know there was any place called (*2) _____

SPEAKER 1: Now, years later, listen to what these people have to say . . .

CHILD 1: Now I love reading and my best friends come to this school. I come to school with some of them, I play here and at home with some of them.

CHILD 2: Thanks to all the help I have had from (*3) _____ I have played for the school (*4) _____ team. I have scored (*5) _____ and (*6) _____

CHILD 3: I have been in the school choir for (*7) _____. We sing on special occasions like the Easter Service, at Christmas, and (*8) _____. We also go on trips to the theatre or concert hall in (*9) _____ to see shows which have singing in them.

CHILD 4: I am in the school recorder group. We play in assembly and on lots of special occasions. We went to give a concert at (*10) _____.

CHILD 5: We've got a computer in our classroom and I get to use it most days. I have written a story on the computer and put some illustrations in it.

CHILD 6: This year I went to (*11) _____. (*12) _____ of us went there for a week with (*13) _____. We had a great time. We saw (*14)_____.

SPEAKER 1: So you see how our six 'rough stones' became much smoother ones by . . .

SPEAKER 2: . . . making friends . . .

SPEAKER 1: . . . learning more about themselves . . .

SPEAKER 2: . . . having the chance to learn more about things like musical instruments and computers . . .

SPEAKER 1: . . . learning the meaning of teamwork . . .

SPEAKER 2: . . . becoming more skilful at things . . .

SPEAKER 1: . . . and learning to be away from home and sharing both fun and responsibilities with others.

CHILD 1: That's right, but we've got to remember who helped us.

CHILD 2: Our teachers, with their skill and knowledge.

CHILD 3: Our parents, who bring us to and from school, and care for us in so many ways.

CHILD 4: The governors who help to make sure the school is running properly.

CHILD 5: The PTA, who help us with so many extra things.

CHILD 1: And the clever people who invented things like pianos, recorders, CD players, televisions and computers.

CHILD 2: And the people who can make these, and mend them for us.

CHILD 3: Architects and builders who designed and built our school.

CHILD 4: Plumbers and electricians who make sure important parts of it work properly.

CHILD 5: The crossing patrol lady who sees that we get here safely.

CHILD 6: The caretaker, cleaners, cooks and helpers who look after us so well here.

SPEAKER 1: Let's sing a hymn to celebrate all these things: hymn number 32, 'Thank you, Lord'.

All the school sing the hymn.

SPEAKER 2: Christian people believe that by following the teachings of Jesus they become better and more 'finished' people.

SPEAKER 1: We will finish our service this morning by reminding you of one of the stories Jesus told.

SPEAKER 2: This story is about a father and his two sons. The father had a large field of grass which he needed cutting so that it would turn into hay . . .

The following short play could be presented in any of these ways:
(a) read by participants;
(b) read by one group, mimed by another;
(c) acted out with words learned previously;
(d) acted out to a tape-recording of the words.

The characters are FATHER, PETER, and PAUL.

FATHER: Right, lads, I want the two of you to be at the field at 8 o'clock tomorrow morning to help me get it cut.

PETER: That's OK with me, Dad. I'll be there at 8 o'clock raring to go. In fact I'm looking forward to it already.

FATHER: What about you, Paul?

PAUL: Well – I've got a lot on tomorrow, Dad – it's a bit difficult to fit it in.

FATHER: Oh – excuses, eh? Why aren't you like your brother? You heard how keen and helpful he is, didn't you?

PAUL: I'm not making excuses, Dad. I really have a lot of things to sort out – but I'll do my very best to be there at 8 o'clock to help out.

FATHER: Humph!

Peter: Don't worry about him, Dad. If he doesn't turn up I'll stay on later to get the job finished. It'll be OK, you'll see.

(Exit all three characters. Enter SPEAKERS 1 and 2.)

SPEAKER 1: So the father went back to his house, and his two grown up sons went to their own houses. Next morning the father was at the field a few minutes before 8 o'clock.

(Enter FATHER.)

FATHER: Well, I thought Peter might already be here, but I'm sure he'll be here by 8 o'clock anyway. As for that Paul . . . hello there's somebody coming up the lane. Hello, Peter . . . oh!

(Enter PAUL.)

PAUL: Hello, father. I'm glad to say I've got everything sorted out. I'm here to help as long as you need me.

FATHER: Oh . . . er right . . . well, Peter will be here any minute now, and we'll finish the work in good time.

PAUL: Well, it's 8 o'clock already. Shall we get started?

FATHER: All right.

SPEAKER 2: The two men started work. Soon it was 8.30 . . . 9 o'clock . . . half past . . . 10 o'clock. The time sped away.

FATHER: I can't understand it. Peter promised he would be here.

PAUL: Ah, but I'm here, Dad, and what's more I'll stay until the job is done.

The assembly could end with the following prayer, read by a teacher.

> This morning we have compared rough stones and smooth stones. As we near the end of another school year we give thanks for the ways in which we have improved – thanks to the help of so many people.
>
> Dear God, teach us always to appreciate the guidance and help we receive. Amen.

The service could then end with the audience departing to the same music as they had heard earlier, on their entry. The significant difference this time, however, is that the piece is allowed to play through without interruption.

4   Saints, everywhere

Aim: To provide more information related to saints, with particular regard to St Margaret.

Materials required: Placards containing the words 'St Albans', a picture of a church, a school, a railway station, a street of houses. Some simple 'dressing up' clothes if the teacher wishes the mimes described in the presentation to be 'costumed'.

Numbers involved: Whole class participation

Calendar location: On or near 10th June

Information and preparation: This is an assembly which has scope for almost limitless adaptation. For instance, if the school is named after a particular saint, or is linked to a church with a specific saint's name, there is obvious scope for more details of these to be added to the assembly.

Similarly, on an appropriate summer morning this assembly could be a little different by being presented out-of-doors instead of in the hall.

Presentation

The introductory music for this assembly should be something in which the word 'Saint' features in the title. This gives considerable scope, ranging from 'For all the Saints', Benjamin Britten's *Saint Nicholas* through to pieces like 'When the saints go marchin' in' and 'St Louis Blues'.

Once the audience is in place, the presenting class could take up position, with all the required visual aids readily to hand. Various speakers might then start things off.

SPEAKER 1: This morning we are going to spend some time talking and thinking about saints.

SPEAKER 2: What is a saint?

SPEAKER 3: One dictionary describes a saint as a person who is very patient and very unselfish.

SPEAKER 4: Saints must certainly be very special. Just look how often we come across the name 'saint'.

(*At this point a group of children with varied visual aids step forward. One of these holds up a placard with ST ALBANS written on it in large letters. She then comments as follows.*)

PLACARD HOLDER 1: You might know somebody who lives in St Albans, or St Annes, or St Davids, or St Andrews. In fact there are almost two hundred towns in Britain whose names begin with 'Saint'.

(*A second presenter steps forward and holds up a placard bearing the picture of a church. This presenter then comments as follows:*)

PLACARD HOLDER 2: Look at my picture of a church. My father was christened in a church called St Bartholomew's; my parents were married in a church called All Saints; my brother was christened in St. Luke's and my cousin was married in St Mary's.

There are hundreds and hundreds of churches all over Britain which are called after Saints.

(*A third presenter from this group steps forward and holds up a placard bearing the picture of a school. This presenter then comments as follows:*)

PLACARD HOLDER 3: Yes – my picture is of a school. You probably know at least one school which is named after a saint. In the town where I live there are four. St Clement's, St Paul's and St Augustine's are all primary schools, and St Mary's is a secondary school.

(*A fourth placard holder steps forward bearing a picture of a railway station:*).

PLACARD HOLDER 4: Other buildings are called after saints too. There is St James's Palace, St Peter's Priory, and St Pancras station!

(*The fifth and last presenter from this group then steps forward to reveal a placard on which a street of houses is shown:*)

PLACARD HOLDER 5: Do you know anybody who lives in a street where the name begins with 'Saint'? This wouldn't be difficult if you lived in London, because you might live in a street named after St Agatha, Agnes, Aidan, Alban, Alfege, Alphage, Alphonsus, Amunds, Andrew, Anne, Anselm, Anthony, Arvan, Asaph, Aubyn, Audrey, Augustine or Austell. There are twenty streets called after a saint whose name starts with the letter A. There are dozens more beginning with the other letters of the alphabet.

(*This placard-bearing group then return to the main body of the*

presenters and the four speakers who started things off step
forward again.)

SPEAKER 1: So, you see there are reminders of saints all around
us.

SPEAKER 2: We're now going to look a little more closely at one
particular saint.

SPEAKER 3: Her name is St Margaret and we're going to tell you
some more about her.

SPEAKER 4: For a start, there are five places in Britain named
after her.

SPEAKER 1: Yes, one of these is St Margaret's Hope in the
Orkney Islands, in the north of Scotland. A strange thing
happened there in the year 1263.

SPEAKER 2: King Haakon IV of Norway sent his ships to invade
the Orkney Islands, but as they sailed into the bay at St.
Margaret's Hope there was an eclipse of the sun.

SPEAKER 3: The sailors thought that this was a warning of things
to come.

SPEAKER 4: They were right. Terrible storms arose and many of
the Norwegians' one hundred and twenty ships were sunk.
Scotland was saved.

SPEAKER 1: Now let us tell you some more about Margaret
herself.

SPEAKER 2: She was born in 1050 and later married King
Malcolm of Scotland. When she was Queen of Scotland,
Margaret did a great many things to help other people. Our
group of actors will show you some of these.

(*At this point the 'acting group' of the presenting class will step
forward and make their presentation. This will have all been
worked out carefully beforehand and will consist of a* NARRATOR
*relating a series of Margaret's good works, while the rest of the
group mime in accordance with the narration. Each pre-arranged
mime could be for as long, or short, as required.*)

NARRATOR: Margaret was a wonderful queen. One of the things
she used to do regularly was to go and sit on a stone, in the open
air, in Dunfermline. There she welcomed people who came to

tell her their troubles and worries. She always took small gifts with her too, and many people were grateful for these.

(*Mimed action.*)

NARRATOR: Another thing Margaret did was to invite crowds of poor and hungry people to come up to the palace. There they were given seats in the great hall and provided with hot food. What's more, the King and Queen served these people personally.

(*Mimed action.*)

NARRATOR: For people who were really desperate, Margaret took even more trouble. She made arrangements for twenty-four people to live at the palace and she herself took care of a little family of orphans.

(*Mimed action to suit this episode. After this the acting group retires to the main body of the presenters and the speakers continue with the assembly.*)

SPEAKER 3: So you see, Margaret set a wonderful example to all who knew her.

SPEAKER 4: She became so famous and well loved that as well as becoming a saint she also became the patroness of Scotland. In England people remember Margaret on her special day on 10th June. In Scotland her day is 16th November.

(*The teacher could now draw the assembly towards its close with the following comments.*)

TEACHER: Reminders of saints are indeed all around us – in our churches, schools, streets, towns and villages. Margaret is just one saint whose life shows us such a fine example of how we might live.

Let us bow our heads and listen to the following prayer:

Dear God, we thank you for the example of your saints. Their patience, unselfishness, their kindness and thoughtfulness to others, their courage and faith, all give us marvellous examples to follow. Amen.

The assembly could then end with everybody singing 'By brother sun' (the song of St Francis, *Come and Praise* Vol 2 No 78).

5   Leavers

Aim: To provide an opportunity for a group of leaving children to show their thoughts about the school and the values they have learned.

Materials required: Individual pieces of work as suggested; appropriate clothing for the gymnastic group; some materials for the shopping scene; twenty to thirty twigs.

Numbers involved: Whole class participation

Calendar location: End of summer term

Information and preparation: This assembly is basically a framework for an end of term leavers' service. The suggestions here could obviously be used, but many teachers and classes will want to amplify them to incorporate material more specifically related to their own situations.

Presentation

The audience could enter to some evocative 'leaving' music, such as 'Auld Lang Syne'. When the presenting class is in place they could begin the assembly with some unison singing, and then address the audience:

CLASS: Soon we will be leaving this school. Today we want to share some of our thoughts about it with you. We have learned lots of things here.

SPEAKER 1: The value of friendship, for one thing. By ourselves we are sometimes worried and lonely – a bit like this twig.

(The speaker produces a single thin twig and breaks it easily.)

SPEAKER 2: When we are all together, in a team, everybody becomes stronger because of this. Look at all these twigs together – they can't be broken so easily.

(The speaker produces a bunch of twenty to thirty twigs, all the same size as the first one. but now in a tight bunch. He/she shows how difficult it is to break the twigs when they are all together like this.)

CLASS: We have learned to read, and this has helped us to understand more things. Listen to this old Chinese poem we have read – it made us think a lot:

When the sun rises I go to work,
When the sun goes down I take my rest.
I dig the well from which I drink,
I farm the soil that yields my food.
I share creation. Kings can do no more.

(*At this point another speaker steps forward and addresses the audience.*)

SPEAKER: We have learned that each of us is different. For instance . . .

(*At this point individual children, and groups, make comments related to their own abilities, and show pieces of their own work:*)

ARTIST: I like painting. I did this picture.

DESIGNERS: We like making models. Here is something we made.

GYMNASTS: We like PE. We are now going to show you some of our skills. (*Appropriate action here.*)

MUSICIAN: I have learned to play the _____ I hope you will enjoy the piece I am going to play. (*Appropriate performance here.*)

MATHEMATICIANS: We like maths. It helps us a lot when we're shopping.

(*Pre-arranged simple shopping scene takes place here with plenty of buying, selling, counting and calculating change.*)

SPEAKER 1: During our time in this school, we have learned the pleasure of doing things together and the need for everybody to appreciate each other's point of view, different ideas and their different skills.

SPEAKER 2: We would like you all to join us in singing: 'And everyone beneath the vine', number 149 in *Come and Praise*.

(*After the singing of the hymn the teacher could conclude proceedings.*)

TEACHER: Let us bow our heads and give thanks for our school and all who work in it. Let us think particularly today of those who are leaving it shortly. May what they have learned here help them to be happy, contented and successful as they take the next step in their lives. Amen.

Section C
Anniversaries, facts
fancies, anecdotes and
religious notes

Many assemblies can be developed from the fertile ground suggested by the above title. This section aims to provide a selection of such starting material.

The summer months

Introduction

Much of the information in this section provides source material for locally developed assemblies. Where a particular event can be linked to an assembly (or assemblies) already detailed in this book, then there is an appropriate note to aid teacher planning.

A note about the various calendars which govern the festivals of different faiths seems important here. *The Gregorian calendar*, which is solar-based and used in most western countries, enables most festivals related to this to be fixed. An Exception is Easter, which is a movable feast. *The Jewish calendar* is lunar-based and to adjust it to the solar year an extra (embolismic) month is added seven times in each nineteen-year period. *The Islamic calendar* is lunar-based without adjustment, which means that Muslim festivals advance by some eleven or twelve days each year. More than one calendar has been in use in India.

The impact of these calendar fluctuations for teachers is that a plan of great religious festivals can only be accurately made by reference to the relevant current calendars. Otherwise it is a question of moving source material about as appropriate.

APRIL

The first half of April is dealt with in *The Spring Assembly Book* in this series. Notes here are for the second half of the month.

16th   Wilbur Wright, the aeroplane inventor and flier, was born in 1867. (*Link – Assemblies 1, 54, 59*)

Marie Tussaud, wax modeller and founder of Madame Tussaud's Waxworks in London, died in 1850. (*See also 26th April.*)

17th   Benjamin Franklin, the often-quoted American statesman and scientist, died on this date in 1790. One of his most appropriate 'sayings' was: 'Do you love life? Then don't squander time, for that is the stuff life is made of.'

This was the date, in 1492, when Columbus set sail to 'discover' the New World. He was equipped with a seal from King Ferdinand of Spain giving him the title of 'Admiral and Viceroy' over all the lands he might discover.

18th   On this night in 1775, Paul Revere rode through the

Massachusetts countryside to warn people that British troops were coming.

This was the date of the San Francisco earthquake in 1906. Devastation and fire caused the death of seven hundred people.

Albert Einstein, the scientist, died in 1955.

19th This is St Alphege's Day. Alphege was the Archbishop of Canterbury when captured by the Danes in the eleventh century. During his captivity he nursed sick Danes who were ill with the plague. He was executed in 1012.

Lord Byron, the poet, died in 1824. Charles Darwin, the naturalist, died in 1882. (*Link – Assemblies 18, 37, 40, 49*)

20th This is the date on which the cuckoo is traditionally first heard in Europe. One old belief associated with this event is that whatever you are doing when you hear its first call – you will be doing most during the rest of the year.

Adolf Hitler was born in 1889.

21st In 753 BC Romulus started to lay the foundations of a city on the banks of the River Tiber. This became Rome. (*Link – Assembly 39*)

Charlotte Brontë, author of *Jane Eyre*, was born in 1816.

Mark Twain (pen name of Samuel Longhorne Clemens) died in 1910. His works included *Tom Sawyer* and *The Adventures of Huckleberry Finn*.

Manfred von Richthofen, the First World War German fighter pilot known as 'the Red Baron', was killed in 1918.

Queen Elizabeth II was born in 1926.

22nd In 1794 Edmund Bon became the first person to qualify as a veterinary surgeon in Great Britain. (*Link – Assembly 36*)

Richard Trevithick, an engineer who pioneered locomotive building in the British Isles, died in 1833.

Yehudi Menuhin, world famous violinist, was born in 1916. (*Link – Assembly 27*)

23rd. Today is St George's Day. ('Cry God for Harry! England and St George!' – from Shakespeare's *Henry V*). The patron saint of England supposedly saved the Libyan town of Sylene from a man-eating dragon. He did this on condition that the inhabitants of the town would be baptised. (*Link – Class Assembly 4*)

This date is also established as Shakespeare's probable date of birth in 1564. He was baptised on the 26th, and died on 23rd April 1616.

William Wordsworth ('I wandered lonely as a cloud . . . saw a crowd, a host, of golden daffodils') died in 1850.

The Pennine Way, the footpath which spans 250 miles (402km) from Derbyshire to the Borders, was opened in 1968. It was Britain's first long-distance footpath.

24th   Daniel Defoe (author of *Robinson Crusoe*) died in 1731.

Joshua Slocum set out in an eleven-metre-long sloop to sail round the world from Boston, USA in 1895. His single-handed journey took three and a half years.

25th   This is St Mark's Day. He died in AD 68, having served as a secretary to the disciple Peter. His writings appear in the Bible under his own name.

Oliver Cromwell was born in 1599.

Work started on the Suez Canal on this date in 1859.

In 1874 Guglielmo Marconi was born in Bologna, Italy. He invented radio telegraphy and was awarded the Nobel Prize for Physics in 1909.

26th   Alfred Krupp, the German industrialist, was born in 1812.

Madame Tussaud's was opened on its current site in London in 1928.

27th   Ferdinand Magellan, the Portuguese explorer, was killed on an expedition in 1521. He named the Pacific Ocean. His ship, which arrived home in Spain in 1522, had completed the first circumnavigation of the world.

Samuel Morse, inventor of the Morse Code, was born in 1791.

Henry Willis, one of Britain's greatest organ builders, was born in 1821. He was also a church organist.

The *Kon-Tiki* expedition set out on its balsawood raft in 1947. (Link – Class Assembly 2)

28th   Captain Bligh of the *Bounty*, together with eighteen men, was set adrift on the ocean in a rowing boat by mutineers led by Fletcher Christian in 1789. He survived to become Governor of New South Wales in Australia.

Lord Shaftesbury (Anthony Ashley Cooper) was born in 1801. He was a great reformer who helped poor children especially. (*Link – Assembly 33*)

29th   Sir Malcolm Sargent, the orchestral conductor, was born in 1895. (*Link – Assembly 38*)

Emperor Hirohito, the 124th of Japan's 'divine' rulers, was born in 1901.

The rose 'Peace' was named on this date in 1945. (*Link – Assembly 31*)

30th   William Lilly was born in 1602. He was one of the first astrologers to become rich and well known for his skills.

Adolf Hitler died in 1945.

Religious notes

While not strictly religious festivals, two important modern Jewish festivals which at the time of writing take place in April are Yom Hashoah which commemorates the victims of the Holocaust, and Yom Ha'atzmant which celebrates Israel's independence.

MAY

May, named after the Roman goddess Maia, could certainly be said to be one of Northern Europe's most popular months. In Britain it is looked upon as the beginning of summer and the month of flowers.

> A trout peeped out
> From his shady nook,
> A butterfly too
> Flew lazily by,
> And the willow catkins
> Shook from on high
> Their yellow dust
> As I passed by:
> And so I know
> That summer is nigh.'
> (Anon.)

1st   This date is celebrated as Labour Day in many countries. Parades and other displays of human achievements are held. (*Link – Class Assembly 1*)

David Livingstone, the Scottish missionary and explorer, died in Africa in 1873. (*Link – Assembly 26*)

This was the date in 1928 when footballer Dixie Dean of Everton and England scored a record number of goals in a season: sixty. (*Link – Assembly 35*)

2nd   This date has an amazing number of connections with flight and flying. (*Link – Assemblies 1, 54, 59*)

Leonardo da Vinci died in 1519.

Baron von Richthofen ('the Red Baron') was born in 1892.

Robert Hewitt began America's first aeroplane passenger service in 1919.

The airship *Hindenburg* left Europe for America on this date in 1937. It exploded when about to land in America and thirty-three people were killed.

The British Overseas Airways Corporation began the first jet airline service in 1952 (England to South Africa).

The spacecraft *Pioneer X* was launched by the USA in 1972. It sent back information about the planet Jupiter.

3rd   In 326 St Helena found the cross on which Jesus was crucified in Jerusalem. *(Link – Assemblies 39, 41, 57, 58)*

The Royal Festival Hall was opened on London's South Bank in 1951.

Margaret Thatcher became Britain's first woman Prime Minister in 1979.

4th   In 1626 Peter Minuit, arriving with four shiploads of settlers and their cattle, reached Manhattan Island, New York. He 'bought' it from the Indians there for some scarlet cloth and brass buttons – valued at $24.

The first Epsom Derby horse race was run in 1780. *(Link – Assembly 28)*.

5th   Napoleon Bonaparte died in 1821.

The first General Strike in Britain's history began in 1926.

Amy Johnson took off for her single-handed flight to Australia in 1930.

Fossils and tools used by men 250,000 years ago were found near Nairobi in Kenya on this date in 1944. *(Link – Assembly 58)*

6th   'Penny Black' stamps were first put on sale on this date in 1840. Some are very valuable, but by no means all are, as millions were printed.

Maria Montessori, the nursery school pioneer, died in 1952. *(Link – Assemblies 56 and 60; Class Assembly 3)*

On the evening of this day in 1954, at Oxford, Roger Bannister became the first man to run a mile in less than four minutes (3 mins 59.4 secs).

7th   Nelson's flag ship, HMS *Victory*, was launched in 1765. It took between two and three thousand oak trees to build it.

Peter Ilich Tchaikovsky, the Russian composer, was born in 1840.

The Second World War in Europe ended when Germany surrendered at 2.41 am on this date in 1945.

In 1959 British Rail announced it was going to close two hundred and thirty BR stations.

In 1979 the age of girls for marriage in Iran was lowered to thirteen years.

8th   Jean Henri Dunant was born in 1828. He founded the International Red Cross and was the first winner of the Nobel Peace Prize (shared with Frédéric Passy), in 1901. Today is World Red Cross Day. (*Link – Assembly 50*)

The Thames Barrier was officially opened in 1984.

9th   This was the date, in 1671, when Thomas Blood, disguised as a priest and with three accomplices, attempted to steal the Crown Jewels. He was captured but pardoned by King Charles II.

John Brown, leader of the anti-slavery movement in America, was born in 1800.

> John Brown's body lies a-moulderin' in the grave,
> But his soul goes marching on.
> (*Link – Assembly 45*)

Tensing Norgay, the Sherpa climber who reached the summit of Mount Everest with Sir Edmund Hillary in 1953, died in 1986.

10th   An eight-day holiday from England to the French Riviera cost £8 in 1938. (Thomas Cook)

US *Triton*, a nuclear submarine, completed a submerged journey round the world in 1961.

11th   Baron Münchhausen was born in 1720. He became famous as a teller of outlandish stories. (*Link – Assembly 29*)

Irving Berlin, writer of more than three thousand popular songs, was born in 1888. His compositions included 'God Bless America' and 'White Christmas'.

In 1941 London endured its worst air raid of the war. Westminster Abbey, St Paul's Cathedral and the British Museum were all damaged and 1,400 people were killed. (*Link – Assembly 12*)

12th   Florence Nightingale was born in 1820. (*Link – Assembly 20*)

> A lady with a lamp I see
> Pass through the glimmering doom.
> (Longfellow)

In 1937 George VI was crowned king. His elder brother Edward VIII had abdicated in 1936.

This date in 1949 marked the end of the Berlin Blockade. The city had been supplied by air since June 1948.

In 1958 it was decided to establish one hundred and sixty square miles of Surrey countryside as an area of outstanding natural beauty. (*Link – Assemblies 18, 37, 40, 49*)

13th   Fridtjof Nansen died in 1930. He was a famous Norwegian

Arctic explorer who later won a Nobel Peace Prize for his welfare work after the First World War. (*Link – Assembly 26*)

14th   In 1796 Edward Jenner established smallpox vaccinations. (*Link – Assemblies 15, 17, 20*)

Henry John Heinz, the American food manufacturer who created '57 varieties' of food products, died in 1919.

In 1948 the new state of Israel was proclaimed.

15th   The Romans celebrated this date as the birthday of Mercury, the messenger of Zeus.

In 1970 Ann Hays and Elizabeth Holsington became the first female generals in the US army.

16th   This is St Brendan's Day. An Irish saint who died in 587, Brendan is believed by some people to have been the first European to have discovered America.

The Woman's Voluntary Service (WVS) was founded in Britain in 1938. In 1966 it became the Women's Royal Voluntary Service.

In 1980 inflation in the United Kingdom reached 21.8%.

17th   Paul Dukas, French composer (*The Sorcerer's Apprentice*) died in 1935.

18th   This is the birthday of Karol Wojtyla – Pope John Paul II. He was born in 1920.

19th   St Dunstan's Day. Dunstan was Archbishop of Canterbury, and a goldsmith, and died in 988. He is credited with devising the coronation service.

Dame Nellie Melba, the famous opera singer, was born in 1861. (*Link – Assembly 21*).

In 1980, Mount St Helens in the USA, a long dormant volcano, erupted killing eight people.

20th   Albrecht Dürer, the painter, was born in 1471. (*Link – Assembly 21*)

Christopher Columbus died in 1506.

Charles Lindbergh flew *The Spirit of St Louis* from New York to Paris – the first solo non-stop flight across the Atlantic. This was in 1929. (*Link – Assemblies 24, 59*)

This was the date, in 1913, of the first Chelsea Flower Show.

The BBC opened its new headquarters in Portland Place in 1932.

The Nature Conservancy Council announced in 1952 that eight areas of England and Scotland were to become nature reserves. (*Link – Assemblies 18, 37, 40, 49*)

21st   There was an earthquake in Britain in 1382. Some churches in

Kent were 'thrown down to the earth' according to *Stow's Chronicle.*

Elizabeth Fry, the prison reformer, was born in 1780.

In 1964 a BBC survey revealed that the Beatles were Britain's most popular tourist attraction.

22nd   Richard Wagner, the composer, was born in 1813. (*Link – Assembly 38*)

Sir Arthur Conan Doyle was born in 1859. (*Link – Assembly 6*)

Victor Hugo died in 1885. His novel *Les Misérables* contains the story of the Bishop's candlesticks which is marvellous assembly material. (*Link – Assembly 55*)

In 1959 the US state of Alabama banned a children's book because it showed a black rabbit marrying a white one.

In 1987 one of Mozart's notebooks was sold for £2.3 million at Sotheby's.

23rd   John D Rockefeller, the American businessman and philanthropist, died in 1937. (*Link – Assembly 45*)

In 1956 it was announced that self-service shops, which were springing up all over Britain, had resulted in quadruple sales. (*Link – Assembly 56*)

24th   Carl Linne, the Swedish naturalist, was born in 1707. He said, 'If a tree dies, plant another in its place.' (*Link – Assembly 37*)

Samuel Morse sent the first message by Morse Code on this date in 1844. It was from Washington to Baltimore, USA and it said, 'What hath God wrought?'

This was the date of a great sea tragedy in 1941. The British battleship HMS *Hood* was hit by a shell from the German ship *Bismarck*. The magazine exploded and only three of the 1,421 men on board survived.

25th   Captain Cook set out on his first voyage of discovery, in the seas around Australia, New Zealand and Indonesia, in 1768.

Igor Sikorsky, designer of the first helicopter in 1939, was born in 1889. (*Link – Assembly 43*)

26th   Samuel Pepys died in 1703. The famous diarist kept his journal from 1660 to 1669 and it encompassed three outstanding events – the Great Plague, the Fire of London and the Dutch attack on the Medway.

Petrol rationing in the UK ended on this date in 1950, five years after the end of the Second World War. (*Link – Assembly 4*)

27th   This is the Feast Day of the Venerable Bede who died at

Jarrow in 735. Known as the Father of the English Church, and a celebrated writer about early Christianity in England, his tomb is in Durham Cathedral. Thought to be the first person to draw up a calendar of the Christian year, he was widely revered in his day. (*Link – Assemblies 15, 30; Class Assembly 4*)

In 1936 the *Queen Mary* (80,773 tons) set sail from Southampton on her maiden voyage.

One of Britain's worst ever road accidents occurred in 1975 when a coach plunged off a road into a ravine in Wharfedale, Yorkshire. Thirty-two people were killed. (*Link – Assembly 4*)

28th This was the birth date of Solomon in 970 BC.

Sir Francis Chichester ended his solo round-the-world voyage on his arrival in Plymouth in 1967. He had completed 15,517 miles and was later knighted by Queen Elizabeth II at Greenwich. She used the sword of Sir Francis Drake for this ceremony. (*Link – Assembly 46*)

29th This is Oak Apple Day – when King Charles II rode into London on his thirtieth birthday in 1660, as newly proclaimed king. He had escaped from Cromwell's army in 1651 by hiding in an oak tree. A traditional old school jingle linked to the day was:

> The twenty-ninth of May
> Is Royal Oak Day;
> If you cannot give us a holiday,
> We'll all run away.

The summit of Mount Everest was reached for the first time on this day in 1953 by Edmund Hillary and Tensing Norgay.

In 1951 eighty-three miners died after an explosion at Easington Colliery in County Durham.

In 1977 Nigel Short (aged eleven) became the youngest ever qualifier in the UK national chess championships. (*Link – Assemblies 22, 43*)

In 1985, rioting in the European Cup Final football match between Liverpool and Juventus at the Heysel Stadium in Brussels resulted in forty-one people being killed.

30th King Arthur is said to have died in 542.

Many historians believe this was the date that Joan of Arc was burned at the stake in Rouen in 1431.

31st This was the date, in 1678, of Lady Godiva's famous naked ride through Coventry. Her husband agreed to remit heavy taxes on the town's people if she did this.

Religious notes

In the Christian Church Ascension Day is the Thursday which is the fortieth day after Easter. This commemorates the last time the disciples saw Jesus before his ascension. This happened on the Mount of Olives and Jesus blessed his followers with the words: 'Lo, I am with you always, even unto the end of the world.' Biblical references for this event are Mark 16, 19; Luke 24–51; Acts 1, 1–11.

There then follow the ten days between Ascension and Whitsun. The latter festival, also known as Pentecost, is the fiftieth day after Easter and celebrates the giving of the Holy Spirit to the followers of Christ. ('Pentecost' comes from the Greek word meaning 'fiftieth'.) It was from this moment that these followers began to preach about Jesus, and therefore it is considered the birthday of the Christian Church. This is also the time which begins the second half of the Christian Year.

This is also the time of the Jewish festival of Shavuoth, which celebrates the giving of the Torah on Mount Sinai. Synagogues are decorated with flowers and plants.

JUNE

June is a month of many associations, including marriage, roses, midsummer, and well dressing. Northern Europeans hope that the weather in reality matches the promise and they can agree with James Lowell's comment: 'What is so rare as a day in June.'

1st   Captain Robert Falcon Scott's ill-fated expedition to the South Pole set out in 1910. (*Link – Assembly 26*)

The *Queen Mary* arrived in New York in 1936 on its maiden voyage.

Helen Keller died in 1968. She was eighty-eight and had become a world-famous lecturer and writer despite being deaf and blind since the age of nineteen months. She was noted for her work with the handicapped. (*Link – Assembly 17*).

2nd   Thomas Hardy, the author, died in 1840.

Queen Elizabeth II was crowned in 1953.

Twenty-nine people were killed in a tremendous explosion which took place at a chemical plant in Flixborough, Humberside, in 1974.

3rd   The game of lacrosse was introduced into Britain in 1876. A group of Canadians gave an exhibition game.

In Japan, this is the day on which a Buddhist ceremony takes place when all broken dolls are taken to priests.

Johann Strauss died in 1899.

4th   In 1913 Emily Wilding Davison, a suffrage campaigner, threw herself in front of the king's horse, Anmer, in the Epsom Derby. She was killed, but her action attracted more attention to the suffrage campaign for the vote for women. (*Link – Assembly 28*)

On this date in 1940 the evacuation was completed of British troops from Dunkirk during the Second World War.

5th   In 1783 Joseph and Etienne Montgolfier gave the first public demonstration of a hot air balloon. This was at Annonay, in the Languedoc in France. The balloon was airborne for ten minutes.

6th   In 1930 frozen peas were sold in America for the first time. That this was possible was due to a 'quick-freeze' technique invented by Clarence Birdseye.

In 1944 the Allied troops landed on the Normandy coast in the D-Day operations.

In 1977 beacons were lit all over the country at the start of Queen Elizabeth II's jubilee celebrations – twenty five years on the throne. (Link – Class Assembly 1)

7th   Robert the Bruce died in 1329. (*Link – Assembly 11*)

Paul Gaugin, the artist, died in 1848.

8th   The prophet Muhammad died in 632. He was the founder of Islam. (*Link – Assemblies 5, 13, 29, 55; Class Assembly 2*)

In 1786 commercially-made ice cream was sold for the first time in New York.

In 1978 Naomi James beat Sir Francis Chichester's record for a solo round-the-world voyage by two days.

9th   This is the feast day of St Columba. He died in 597 and is considered the spreader of the gospel over the northern part of the British Isles. (*Link – Assembly 30*)

George Stephenson, inventor of railways, was born in 1781.

Charles Dickens died in 1870. Queen Victoria said of him, 'He is a very great loss. He had a large and loving mind.'

In 1958 Queen Elizabeth opened the new and improved facilities at Gatwick Airport. (*Link – Assembly 24*).

10th   Feast day of St Margaret (b. 1050) in England. (*Link – Class Assembly 4*)

The first World Cup Soccer Final was played in Rome in 1934. The score was Italy 2, Czechoslovakia 1.

The 'biro', a ball point pen, was patented by Hungarian Laszlo Biro in 1943.

The 750th anniversary of the signing of the Magna Carta was celebrated in St Paul's Cathedral in 1965.

11th   This is the feast day of St Barnabas. He accompanied St Paul on his gospel-spreading journeys and is believed to have been put to death for his beliefs in Cyprus.

John Constable, the painter, was born in 1776.

Britain's first North Sea oil was pumped ashore in 1975. (*Link – Assembly 45*)

In 1982 forty-two British soldiers were killed in the fighting at Fitzroy in the Falklands War.

12th   Auguste and Louis Lumière showed the first newsreel film in Paris in 1895. Many among the audience were frightened by its realism.

Bryan Allen 'pedalled' across the Channel in a pedal powered aircraft in 1979. The flight took three hours.

In 1980 Billy Butlin, the founder of Britain's popular holiday camps, died aged eighty. (*Link – Assembly 56*).

13th   The Virgin Mary, mother of Jesus, died in AD 40.

St Anthony, patron saint of the illiterate, died in 1231.

The MCC was founded in 1787. (*Link – Assembly 35*)

Jesse Boot, Lord Trent, founder of Boots the Chemist, died in 1931.

In 1956 Real Madrid won soccer's first European Cup, beating Stade de Reims, 4–3.

14th   Captain Bligh, set adrift from the *Bounty*, arrived in Timor in 1789. With the barest of supplies, he and his eighteen companions had completed a journey of 3,618 miles in an open boat.

This is Flag Day in the USA – to commemorate the adoption of the 'Stars and Stripes' as the national flag in 1777.

The first non-stop flight of the Atlantic was made by William Alcock and Arthur Whitten-Brown in 1919.

John Logie Baird, who pioneered the invention of the television, died in 1946 aged fifty-eight.

In 1961 push-button controlled pedestrian crossings were introduced into Britain. (*Link – Assembly 47*)

15th   World Children's Day.

This is St Vitus's Day. This fourth-century saint and martyr is the patron of actors and dancers.

In 1215 King John signed the Magna Carta – the first documentation of human freedom. (*Link – Assembly 50*)

Benjamin Franklin proved the existence of electricity in lightning in 1752. This was done by flying a kite in a storm. It was struck by lightning and the electricity ran down it to make a spark near the ground. (*Link – Assembly 22*)

In 1952 Anne Frank's diary was published. She had kept it from 1942 to 1944, before her family was discovered and sent to a concentration camp. (*Link – Assembly 31*)

16th Henry Ford founded the Ford Motor Company in Detroit, USA, in 1903.

General William Bramwell Booth, founder of the Salvation Army, died in 1929.

Edmund Hillary and John Hunt received knighthoods for their parts in the successful 1953 Mount Everest expedition.

In 1963 Russia put the first woman in space when Lieutenant Valentina Tereshkova circled the earth in a *Vostok* spacecraft. She was twenty-six.

17th John Wesley, the founder of Methodism, was born in 1703. Wesley preached thousands of sermons all over the country. He travelled mainly on horseback, lived abstemiously and gave away an estimated £30,000 in his lifetime. ('Give all you can'). (*Link – Assemblies 14, 21, 23*)

18th The Battle of Waterloo took place in 1815. This finally ended the ambitions of Napoleon, who abdicated on 22nd June and was banished to St Helena. (*Link – Assembly 31*)

19th The French genius Blaise Pascal was born in 1623. A brilliant mathematician (he invented a digital calculator, and a syringe) he was also a very religious man and a philosopher. 'If you want people to think well of you, do not speak well of yourself.' (*Link – Assembly 42*)

James Barrie (author of *Peter Pan*) died in 1937.

In 1961 archeological evidence relating to Pontius Pilate was found a few miles from Haifa in Caesarea, Israel. A stone slab was discovered on which were two names: Pontius Pilate and Emperor Tiberius. (*Link – Assembly 41; Class Assembly 1*)

In 1978 Ian Botham achieved England's greatest all-round performance in a cricket test match. This was against Pakistan at Lords, when he scored a century and had bowling figures of 8–34. He was twenty-two at the time. (*Link – Assembly 35*)

20th This day in 1837 saw Queen Victoria's accession to the British throne. Her coronation was held on 28th June 1838.

The medal, the Victoria Cross, was created in 1856. The first person to be awarded it was Lieutenant Charles Lucas who threw a live bomb off a ship's deck. It exploded immediately. (*Link – Assembly 54*)

21st   This is the longest day of the year in the northern hemisphere (except on leap years)

22nd   In 1923 runaway inflation meant that there were 622,000 German marks to the £1.

        On this date in 1941 Germany invaded Russia in the Second World War. (*Link – Assembly 31*)

        In 1964 Francis Chichester set a new solo boat crossing of the Atlantic in under thirty days.

        In 1970 it was announced by the Methodist Church that women would be recognised as full ministers.

23rd   In 1683 William Penn arranged the signing of a treaty between settlers and indigenous people in the State of Pennsylvania. This established peace in the state – something very different from other states in America. (*Link – Assembly 8*)

24th   This is John the Baptist's Day. This is unusual in that the Christian Church usually celebrates saints on the day of their death – not so in John's case. (*Link – Assembly 41*)

        This is Midsummer Day.

        Keith Castle was Britain's longest surviving heart transplant patient until he died this day in 1985. He had lived for six years with his new heart.

25th   This was the date of 'Custer's Last Stand' in 1876. At a battle by the Little Big Horn River in Montana Custer's force was wiped out by Sioux Indians.

        The Korean War began in 1950.

26th   According to legend, in 1284 the Pied Piper lured away one hundred and thirty children from the German town of Hamelin. This was because the town fathers refused to honour his fee of 1,000 guilders for ridding the town of rats. (*Link – Assembly 3*)

        Delegates from fifty states met in San Francisco to sign the World Security Charter in 1945. This was to establish an international peace-keeping body called the United Nations.

27th   Helen Keller was born in 1880.

28th   Queen Victoria was crowned at Westminster in 1838.

        Archduke Franz Ferdinand, heir to the throne of Austria-Hungary, and his wife were assassinated in Sarajevo. The assassin was a Serb called Gavrilo Princip and the act was to contribute to the outbreak of the First World War.

        Prince William was born in 1982.

29th   St Peter, the disciple, was crucified in 68. (Link – Class Assembly 4)

The Automobile Association was founded in 1905. The annual membership then was two guineas. (*Link – Assembly 4*)

In 1925 a law was passed in South Africa banning all black people from holding skilled jobs.

In 1968 Britain's first credit card – the Barclaycard – was introduced.

30th   Tower Bridge was opened by the Prince of Wales in 1894.

In 1938 a new comic appeared in the USA – *Superman*.

In 1948 this was the date the Berlin Airlift began. The beleaguered city was supplied entirely by air.

Religious notes

At the time of writing the Muslim *Hajj* takes place in early June. (Its Islamic location is from 8th to 13th Zul-Hijja.) This is the time when Muslims from all over the world make their pilgrimage to the Sacred Mosque at Mecca in Saudi Arabia. Every Muslim seeks to make this pilgrimage once in a lifetime.

Simple clothing is worn by all. Pilgrims make seven circuits of the Ka'aba; they may also make seven journeys between the two hills of Safa and Marwah nearby. Mount Arafat is visited. Sacrifices are made; the men's heads are shaven and women have a lock of hair cut off. Time is spent in prayer and meditation.

At the time of writing, the Muslim festival of Eid-ul-Adha is celebrated in early June. This is a festival of sacrifice when Muslims give meat to the poor, and send presents of meat to friends and relatives.

At the time of writing, the important Buddhist festival of Wesak (Vaisakhapuja) also takes place in early June. This commemorates the birth, enlightenment and death of Buddha. There are pageants and candlelit processions.

At the time of writing, the Muslim festival of Hijrat (New Year) falls in late June (1st Muharran). This commemorates the occasion when the Prophet and his followers left Mecca and were welcomed in Medina in 622.

The Christian feast of Corpus Christi ('the body of Christ') is celebrated on the Thursday after Whit week. It commemorates the institution of the Eucharist at the Last Supper.

JULY

'Then came hot July, boiling like to fire'.

So said Edmund Spenser, but as well as its reputation for heat, this month has strong links with wet weather as it contains St Swithin's Day. It was Mark Antony who named the month in honour of Julius Caesar; the Anglo-Saxon name, 'Hey Monath', simply reflected the time of hay harvesting.

1st   Prince Charles became the Prince of Wales in 1969.

Louis Blériot, the French airman who made the first flight across the English Channel, was born in 1872.

2nd   Nostradamus, the astrologer and prophet, died in 1566.

In 1964 the Civil Rights Act was signed in the USA. This was intended to prevent racial discrimination of any kind. (*Link – Assembly 13*)

3rd   This is the beginning of the period known to the Romans as 'the dog days' (3rd July to 11th August). The name derives from the fact that the Dog Star (Canicular) rose at this time. These days were considered the hottest of the year, when 'dogs grew mad, other animals languid and men prey to fevers, hysterics and frenzies'.

4th   This is Independence Day in the USA. The Declaration of Independence was made in 1776 and contained some memorable phrases, notably: 'We hold these truths to be self evident, that all men are created equal . . . ' (*Link – Assembly 2*)

Thomas Barnardo was born in 1845. It was while training to be a medical missionary in London that the Irishman discovered the orphans that led to his work with Dr Barnardo's homes. (*Link – Assembly 33*)

In 1968 Alec Rose, aged fifty-nine, completed his solo round-the-world voyage when he returned to Portsmouth. His boat was *The Lively Lady* and he had sailed her 28,500 miles in 354 days.

5th   Sir Thomas Stamford Raffles, founder of Singapore, died in 1826.

The first Thomas Cook excursion took place in 1841 (from Leicester to Loughborough). (*Link – Assemblies 4, 56*)

Phineas T. Barnum, the circus proprietor and presenter of the 'The Greatest Show on Earth', was born in 1810.

In 1952 this was the last date on which trams ran in London.

6th   Sir Thomas More, Chancellor of England, was executed in 1535 because he refused to sanction the marriage of Henry VIII to Anne Boleyn. He was canonised in 1935, and the 6th is now his feast day.

        Louis Armstrong, the jazz trumpeter and singer, died in 1971. His song 'Black and Blue' provides thought-provoking assembly material for top juniors.

7th   Another 'first' in Channel crossings took place on this date in 1981. Stephen Ptacek made the first solar-powered flight.

        Sir Arthur Conan Doyle, creator of Sherlock Holmes, died in 1930.

8th   La Fontaine, French writer of stories and 'thoughts for the day', died in 1621. His material is still a richly rewarding source for assemblies. (*Link – Assemblies 8, 14, 19, 23, 25, 32, 42, 47, 51, 55*)

9th   Edward Heath, the former British Prime Minister and advocate of European Union, was born in 1916.

        The seven-hundred-year-old York Minster was hit by a bolt of lightning in 1984. The ensuing fire caused over a million pounds worth of damage. (*Link – Assembly 22*)

10th   The Emperor Hadrian died in 138. Hadrian's Wall covers a distance of seventy-three miles across the north of England.

        A survey in 1951 discovered that British housewives worked a seventy-five-hour week.

11th   Robert the Bruce, King of Scotland, was born in 1274.

12th   Julius Caesar was born in 100 BC.

        George Eastman, the photographer, inventor of roll films and cheap cameras, and founder of Kodak, was born in 1854.

13th   Bertrand de Guesclin, 'the founder of French chivalry', knight and statesman, died in 1380. (*Link – Assemblies 7, 9*)

14th   Bastille Day. This is a national holiday in France and commemorates the storming of the Bastille Prison in 1789. It marked the beginning of the Revolution and is a symbol of the victory of democracy over aristocratic rule.

        Emmeline Pankhurst, the suffrage leader who organised the Women's Social and Political Union, died in 1928.

15th   Feast of St Swithin, who died in 862. (*Link – Assembly 55*)

        In 1945, after more than two thousand nights of official 'black-out' during the war, lights came on again all over Britain.

        Officially the beginning of the Muslim age in 622. (*Link – Assemblies 5, 13, 29, 55; Class Assembly 2*)

16th   In 1439, in an effort to stop the spreading of plague germs, kissing was banned in England. (*Link – Assembly 20*)

Roald Amundsen, the Norwegian explorer and navigator who was the first man to reach the South Pole, was born in 1872.

17th   St Alexius's Day. Alexius, having left home, returned in disguise to live under his father's rule as a servant as badly treated as his peers. He revealed his identity just before he died.

In 1981 Queen Elizabeth II opened the Humber Estuary Bridge – a total length of 1.37 miles.

18th   WG Grace, the legendary cricketer who scored of 54,896 runs, including 126 centuries, and took 2,876 first-class wickets, was born in 1848. (*Link – Assembly 35*)

In 1955 Disneyland was opened in California, USA.

19th   This is the feast day of St Vincent de Paul, carer for galley slaves, whose story makes very good assembly material. (*Link – Assembly 39*)

The first Wimbledon Lawn Tennis Championships were held in 1877.

20th   This was the date, in 1969, when men – Neil Armstrong and Edwin Aldrin – landed on the moon for the first time.

21st   Ancient Egyptians believed the world was created on this day.

Daniel Lambert, recorded as England's fattest ever man, died in 1809. He weighed 739 pounds (approximately 336 kilos).

22nd   The Reverend William Spooner, a nervous speaker, became famous for his 'Spoonerisms'. One example was: 'Sir, you have tasted two whole worms.' (Sir, you have wasted two whole terms.) He was born on this day in 1844 and served both as dean and later warden of New College, Oxford.

The World Health Organisation was founded in 1946. (*Link – Assembly 20*).

23rd   In 1904 Charles E Menches of St Louis, USA, thought of a new way to serve ice cream – in a cone.

24th   Alexandre Dumas, author of *The Three Musketeers*, was born in 1802.

Captain Webb, the first man to swim the English Channel (in 1875), drowned while attempting to swim Niagara Falls in 1883.

25th   This is the feast day of St James, disciple of Jesus and elder brother of St John. He was martyred in 44. This is also St Christopher's Day. He is the patron saint of travellers and is symbolised by a palm-tree staff. (*Link – Assembly 57; Class Assembly 4*)

The English Channel was crossed for the first time by plane in 1909 (the pilot was Louis Blériot). On the same day in 1959 the first Hovercraft crossing was made.

26th   This is the feast day of St Anne, the mother of the Virgin Mary. (*Link – Class Assembly 4*)

John Wilmont, Earl of Rochester, a poet and wit, and leader of the court of King Charles II, said of the king: ' . . . never says a foolish thing; nor ever does a wise one.'

27th   Tradition has it that this was the day Noah sent the dove out of the ark. (*Link – Assembly 3*)

Jim Laker took the most wickets ever in a cricket test match. This was nineteen – for England against Australia at Old Trafford, Manchester, in 1956.

28th   Johann Sebastian Bach, the composer, died in 1750.

Hans Andersen, the Danish author, died in 1875. (*Link – Assembly 3*)

In 1964 Sir Winston Churchill, then eighty-nine, made his last appearance in the House of Commons.

29th   The Spanish Armada was defeated in 1588.

William Wilberforce, the social reformer, died in 1833. One month after his death the Slavery Abolition Act was passed by Parliament. (*Link – Assembly 33*)

In 1981 Prince Charles married Lady Diana Spencer.

30th   Henry Ford, of motorcar fame, was born in 1863.

In 1966 England won the World Soccer Cup for the first time when they defeated Germany 4–2 at Wembley.

31st   This is the feast day of St Ignatius Loyola. He founded the order of the Jesuits and wrote one of the most famous prayers of all time:

Teach us, good Lord, to serve thee as thou deservest; to give and not to count the cost; to fight and not to heed the wounds; to toil and not to seek for rest; to labour and not to ask for any reward save that of knowing that we do thy will.

Religious notes

At the time of writing the Muslim Ashura, which is celebrated on the tenth day of Muharram, falls in early July. This day commemorates the time God saved Moses from the pursuit of the Pharaoh and the Prophet decreed it a day of fasting to remember this, and the tragedies which beset Muhammad's family.

Tish B'ar is a Jewish day of mourning in mid July. The Book of Lamentations is read as a reminder of the destruction of the first and second temples in Jerusalem, and other tragedies in Jewish history.

Section D
Assemblies linked
by theme

This section seeks to aid teachers who wish to present a number of assemblies linked by themes which are popular ones in a primary school and RE context. No assembly story from the book has been used more than three times in the groupings which follow. The assemblies are shown by their number and title.

Animals

  6 How did they do it?
 11 It's not fair
 16 The grave
 18 This month (May)
 19 Getting what you deserve
 25 Once too often
 28 The cheat
 36 Keep on trying
 40 This month (June)
 42 Six wise men?
 47 Be prepared
 49 This month (July)
 51 Stick together
 52 Rumours
 58 Underground treasure

Concern

  1 The mystery
  8 I don't like you
 11 It's not fair
 12 James Merryweather
 15 Christian Aid week

 20 Thank you, doctor
 26 Julie's story
 28 The cheat
 31 Peace is best
 32 The cooking pot
 33 Sarah Gooder's story
 50 What can I do to help?

Courage

  1 The mystery
  4 A day out
 17 Determination
 26 Julie's story
 39 An early hero
 41 John
 43 To the rescue
 48 One of Scotland's brave
 54 Teamwork
 59 All alone

Class assembly:

  4 Saints, everywhere

Section E

The stories

This section classifies the stories according to source categories – *folk*, *true*, *religious*, *original* or *contemporary* – for teachers who wish to use them in groupings of this nature. The assemblies are shown by their numbers and titles.

Folk stories, myths, legends

8   I don't like you
11 It's not fair
14 Enough is enough
16 The grave
19 Getting what you deserve
23 Fair shares
25 Once too often
29 A wise man
32 The cooking pot
42 Six wise men?
46 The traveller's gift
47 Be prepared
51 Stick together

True stories

1   The mystery
4   A day out
6   How did they do it?
7   Milkman extraordinary
9   Crane rescue
12 James Merryweather
15 Christian Aid week
17 Determination
18 This month (May)
20 Thank you, doctor
22 Lightning strike
24 Mayday!
26 Julie's story
28 The cheat
31 Peace is best
33 Sarah Gooder's story
36 Keep on trying
37 Trees
38 A life to treasure
40 This month (June)
43 To the rescue
45 Rich as Rockefeller
48 One of Scotland's brave
49 This month (July)
50 What can I do to help?
54 Teamwork
59 All alone

Religious stories

3   Jonah
5   Trust in Allah
13 Leading the way

Section F
National Curriculum
cross-references

This section is intended as a guide for teachers who wish to integrate these assemblies into other areas of the National Curriculum. The assemblies are shown by their number and title, listed under the appropriate subject headings.

Art

12 James Merryweather
16 The grave
21 The sisters
29 A wise man
37 Trees
39 An early hero
40 This month (June)
42 Six wise men?
46 The traveller's gift
48 One of Scotland's brave
52 Rumours
57 The traveller's friend

Class assemblies

1 Let's celebrate
5 Leavers

English

All the stories in this book could be incorporated into some aspect of English work – discussion, drama, expressing opinions, writing creatively and descriptively.

Geography

3 Jonah
5 Trust in Allah
6 How did they do it?
8 I don't like you
10 The move
11 It's not fair
12 James Merryweather
13 Leading the way
14 Enough is enough
15 Christian Aid week
16 The grave
19 Getting what you deserve
20 Thank you, doctor
22 Lightning strike
24 Mayday!
25 Once too often
27 Down and out?
29 A wise man
30 Getting over a bad start

Section G
Resources

Addresses

SAEs are welcomed when you contact the following addresses, which are useful for specially produced material.

General

Save the Children, Mary Datchelor House, 17 Grove Lane, London SE5 8SP. (The magazines are a constant source of excellent assembly stories.)

The RE Centre, National Society (Church of England) for Promoting Religious Education, 23 Kensington Square, London W8 5HN. The Centre distributes the annual journal of the SHAP Working Part on World Religions in Education, which is particularly valuable for precise annual dates of religious festivals.

SHAP teachers' information service: Vida Barnett, 81 St Mary's Road, Huyton, Merseyside L36 5SR.

Independent Publishing Company, 38 Kennington Lane, London SE11 4LS. They publish a large selection of books, posters and cards relating particularly to South-East Asian countries.

Christianity

Christian Education Movement, Royal Buildings, Victoria Street, Derby DE1 1GW. By subscribing to the CEM schools receive a termly mailing of material which is always useful for RE, and sometimes specially aimed at assemblies.

Hinduism

Hindu Centre, 7 Cedars Road, London E15 4NE.

ISCON Educational Services, Bhakti Vedanta Manor, Letchworth, Hetfordshire WD2 8ED.

Islam

Iqra Trust, 24 Culross Street, London W1Y 3HE.

Muslim Educational Trust, 130 Stroud Green Road, London N4 3RZ.

Judaism
Jewish Education Bureau, 8 Westcombe Avenue, Leeds L58 2BS.

Books and stories

One of the difficulties of recommending books is that, particularly in recent years, titles have either gone out of print or changed publishers at a bewildering rate.

The wise teacher therefore will seek to build up a range in two areas. The first of these would be the background-information type of book, including material like *Celebrations*, a series of booklets by Maurice Lynch (Ginn). Other most useful sources are: *Festival*, a series of booklets by Olivia Bennett (Commonwealth Institute and Macmillan); *Festivals and Saints' Days* by V Green (Blandford); Black's *Bible Dictionary* (A & C Black).

The second collection will consist of folk tales which often produce marvellous assembly material. New anthologies appear with great regularity and should always be examined carefully. Old favourites like *Anansi*, the *Hodja, Brer Rabbit* and Aesop's *Fables* are suitable for many re-tellings and adaptations.

A very good way to find out about new and useful books in this field is to subscribe to *Books for Keeps*, a magazine of children's books (6 Brightfield Road, London SE12 8QF).

A book of anniversaries is always useful. The *Longman History of the 20th Century* is a marvellous source. It is usually 'for reference only' in public libraries but is an invaluable addition to any school's reference library. Another book recommended for the library is *Dates and Meanings of Religious Festivals* by J Walshe (Foulsham).

Newspapers provide an endless supply of stimulating true stories, and the advantage of local newspapers is that they often have appropriate stories which have taken place in settings familiar to the children.

Teachers should not neglect Asian-owned newsagencies either. These are useful sources for items such as festival cards and Hindu legends in comic-strip form.

Resources for music

The BBC'S *Come and Praise* anthologies are the source for all the hymns recommended in this book. It would be hard to better this series for primary hymns.

Festivals by Jean Gilbert (Oxford University Press, Music

Department, Walton Street, Oxford OX2 6DP) is a very useful anthology with suggestions for songs and musical activities related to festivals.